Write Your Own Business Case Studies

Plus Media Releases, Articles, Blogs, eblasts, and Handouts for a Complete Marketing Campaign

With the rise of social media, now, more than ever, companies and consumers make their buying decisions based on word-of-mouth recommendations. Testimonials now play a stronger role in our marketing materials. Case studies take this a step further by providing instant credibility for your company, products, and services.

Fortune 500 corporations have included case studies on their sites for years and companies around the globe are following suit.

If you've chosen to join this wave and would like to write a marketing-styled business case study, whether it's for your own company or as a freelance writer, welcome to this step-by-step guide.

This book guides you through the topic selection process, interviewing, structuring the case study, and in-depth writing and editing instruction.

When the case study is done – you'll hold onto your notes because this is just the beginning. With the hard work behind you in research and interviewing, you're set to expand your marketing portfolio in part two of the book with handouts, media releases, eblasts, articles, and blogs.

Let's get started!

Write Your Own Business Case Studies

Plus Media Releases, Articles, Blogs, eblasts,
and Handouts
for a Complete Marketing Campaign

Paula Wheeler

Knight Vision Productions

Knight Vision Productions
Learn It – Do It book series
www.knight-vision.com
www.learnit-doit.com

© 2011 Paula C. Wheeler

All rights reserved. Permission is granted to copy or reprint the *Case Study Template* and *10 Tips to Strengthening Your Writing*, for personal use only. No other parts of the book may be reproduced or transmitted in any form, including electronic, online, or photocopying with the exception of brief passages for reviews to be printed without written permission from the author.

Case studies, stories, and examples are fictional and do not represent any clients or other persons or businesses. Although the author has prepared the manuscript with care and makes every effort to ensure accuracy, she takes no responsibility for errors, omissions, or inaccuracies. The author offers general information that is not intended to render legal advice.

Cover design by Sapo Creative Studios – www.sapo.ca

ISBN: 978-0-9866207-0-6

Library and Archives Canada Cataloguing in Publication
Wheeler, Paula Clare
    Write your own business case studies : plus media releases, articles, blogs, eBlasts, and handouts for a complete marketing campaign / Paula Wheeler.
Includes index.
ISBN 978-0-9866207-0-6

    1. Marketing–Case studies. 2. Business writing. I. Title.
HF5415.13.W44 2011   658.80072'2   C2011-901261-8

Library of Congress subject headings:
Marketing
Business writing
Management—Case studies—Study and teaching

Write Your Own Business Case Studies – First Edition

Table of Contents

Introduction 9
   What's in the Book? 10
   Why Did I Write a Book on Business Case Studies? 11

1: What is a Case Study? 13
   Why Use Case Studies? 13
   Where Do You Use Case Studies? 14
   What Copywriters Know to Give Them an Edge 16

2: Choose Your Case Study 19
   Your Readers...Do You Know Who They Are? 20
   Who Will Write Your Case Study? 20
   Finding Clients and Topics 22
   Getting to Yes 23
   CAUTION: When "Yes" Goes Bad 24
   Research 25

3: Structure the Case Study 27
   The Case Study and Classic Story Structure 27
      Act One 30
      Act Two 33
      Act Three 38

Table of Contents

4: The Template 41
    Introduction to the Case Study Template 41
    Case Study Template 42

5: The Customer Interview 47
    Customer Sign-Off 48
    Preparation 49
    Making the Interview Call 50
    The Transcript 54
    The Recording 55

6: Prepare to Write 57
    Highlight the Important Information 57
    Use Quotations 59
    Make Every Word Count 63
    Tighten Your Writing 64
    Use All the Senses 64
    One Last Check of Your Audience 66

7: Write the Case Study 67
    Writing the First Words 67
    Headlines and Subheads 68
    Write a Masterful Headline 70

8: Polish Your Prose 75
    Surviving the Revision Cycle 75
    Ten Tips for Strengthening Your Writing 78

9: Trade Show & Sales Handouts 93

10: Media Releases 95
    Attracting the Editor's Attention 95
    Attracting and Holding the Reader's Attention 96
    Why Write a Media Release? 96
    What is the Goal of Your Media Release? 99
    How to Format Your Media Release 101
    The Media Release Backgrounder and Fact Sheet 108

11: e-mails and eblasts 109
Why Use Them? 109
Solicited and Unsolicited e-mails and eblasts 109
Building a List 110
Use Opt-in Forms to Create a List 111
Use e-mails and eblasts to Your Advantage 112
Target Companies with Personalized Correspondence ... 113
Using Your Case Study in an e-mail or eblast 114

12: Articles 115
For Newsletters, Magazines, and Advertorials 115
Why Write an Article? 115
Writing to Your Audience 116
Structuring the Article 117
Writing the Article 119
Newsletters 124
Aiming at Magazines and ezines 126
Advertorials 131

13: Blogs 137
The Purpose of Using a Blog in Your Marketing 137
Create the Atmosphere 138
Audience 140
Structure – From a Marketing Perspective 140
Advertising 142
Using Your Case Study Material in a Blog 142
Keeping the Content Fresh 143
In Conclusion 145

Appendix I – A Word on Testimonials 147

Appendix II: Case Study Samples 149
Case Study Samples 150
Shortening Your Case Study 158
Switching to Advertising Language 165

Index 167

Introduction

I've had the great fortune to work with many dozens of writers over the years. Some were book authors, some professional business writers, but for the most part, they were project managers, marketing executives, and administrative staff in companies from one person to several thousand people. Their goal was the same. They wanted my help in writing, revising, or polishing a document before it was published.

In every instance, I looked at the underlying structure first, then worked my way up to the finished product. Think about any building project and you'll see why. Without a sturdy foundation, the whole thing comes crashing down.

In *Write Your Own Business Case Studies*, I'll show you a structure for developing case studies and five other collateral marketing pieces that is so inherent to you, you'll wonder why you never thought of it before.

> **Case Studies**
> Written in one or two pages (three at most!), a marketing-styled business case study is the story of a third party's successful interaction with your company. No amount of paid advertising creates as much credibility as this long-form testimonial.

Introduction

By using proven story structure techniques, you'll capture and hold your readers' attention while you lightly infuse your selling pitch.

Whatever your reason for choosing this book, you'll find everything you need to research, interview, structure, and write a publishable case study plus five other documents to round-out your marketing campaign.

What's in the Book?

Part One – Writing Case Studies

As case studies increase in popularity among businesses, the price for hiring a professional to write one also increases. Using our comprehensive template for interviewing and writing, you could save $500 - $1500 on professional writing fees, per case study, by writing them yourself.

Here's what you'll cover:

- Choosing a topic
- Structuring the case study
- Making the customer interview
- Working with the template
- Tips for writing and editing the study

Good news for freelancer writers too. Add case study writing to your portfolio of work and tap into this expanding market.

Part Two – Five Ways to Spin a Case Study for Your Marketing Portfolio

Why spend your time and efforts on data collection, interviewing, and document structure for one document – when you can write your full campaign?

Why Did I Write a Book on Business Case Studies?

In this section you'll learn how to top-up your marketing packages with five additional documents based on the material you've already gathered or written.

Here's what you'll cover:

- Handouts for trade shows and sales folders
- Media Releases
- Articles and advertorials for magazines, e-zines, and newsletters
- Blog posts
- e-mails / eblasts

Why Did I Write a Book on Business Case Studies?

I started my business in 1998, but it wasn't until three years later I was asked to write a case study. I remember feeling like a rookie all over again. Texts and reference books taught a drier case study style – with analyses and recommendations. Clearly this wasn't what my customer wanted when she said they'd use it as a marketing tool for their product.

Then I came across a few small articles that opened a new world on case studies. These kept the challenge-approach-results formula but used a more conversational language style. I felt as though I were reading a story instead of a case study.

This relaxed approach gained popularity and soon it was popping up on the websites of large corporations everywhere. Still, I found little in the way of in-depth writing instruction for these important marketing documents. And that's exactly what they've come to be in today's business world.

Hence, this book.

For the professional writer who is unfamiliar with the case study format or the non-professional who wants to submit a

Introduction

polished document, *Write Your Own Business Case Studies* takes you through the standard format for case studies using the same story structure we've come to know in books, television shows, and movies. Add that to the template I've provided to guide you through the must-have information in each section, and you'll have a case study written before you have time to worry about writing one.

Enjoy the adventure!

Paula Wheeler

> **BONUS** – Frequent updates to websites and blogs increase their search engine optimization (SEO). Are you aiming for page-one placement? Keep your case studies and blog updated often to help your company climb the ranks.

Part One

1: What is a Case Study?

Case studies are high-octane testimonials – and they're free for the asking.

As an invaluable sales document, a case study hands readers your company's success stories from the viewpoint of your client. Where else can you find this kind of credibility for your product or service claims?

Business case studies today have evolved from the longer drier versions of their predecessors, yet they still follow the proven document structure your readers know. They target the fast-paced, need-to-be-entertained audience but cater to the typical time-restraints of the average business person. And when they follow a story structure your reader inherently recognizes as well, your product and service is remembered more vividly (and with more interest) than a sales sheet filled with features and benefits.

Why Use Case Studies?

Let's say you're in the market for a new photocopier. You start researching brands and models and look for credible information to help you come to a decision. Who are you more likely to believe…a sales rep from the copier company or a customer

1: What is a Case Study?

of theirs you've met over lunch? Would the marketing pitch in a glossy brochure lead you to call them – or the *verifiable* testimonial tucked along its sidebar?

If you prefer personal feedback, you're in good company.

- Case studies are the **most highly read** of all marketing materials. Think of them as the older, wiser cousins of the testimonial.
- They're more **in-depth** than a testimonial. (It's a proven marketing technique that longer sales copy sells better than short letters and ads. Really! It's true!)
- Case studies show a **real solution for a real customer's problem** and how that customer stands behind his decision. (The best kind of credibility!)
- They're in a recognized format with an easy-to-read style that helps **readers remember** the details.
- The product is highlighted by being **in context with a real life situation**.
- They're the least expensive and **most credible advertising** you'll do.
- They zero-in on one subject – **one challenge** – giving readers an in-depth look, and leaving you with more areas to explore on the same product for future case studies. (Specifics sell.)

Where Do You Use Case Studies?

Case studies are one of the most versatile components of your marketing materials. Published as-is or adjusted to suit other mediums, case studies give your message wide exposure without inventing new material.

Websites: These are the most popular form of distribution and partly why case studies have a lower word-count from their

Where Do You Use Case Studies?

earlier counterparts. They've also become more conversational in tone. Web visitors give your site five or six seconds to grab their attention – then you have to maintain it. Long blocks of text won't be read. Show visitors a catchy first line from a case study as a link on your home page and they're on their way!

Handouts and inserts for trade shows, sales packages, presentations, RFPs, and proposals: Case studies of a page or two are perfect for two-sided handouts. The shorter the case study the more likely it will be read. If you have room to leave large margins and add photos, readership will be even higher.

Where Do You Use Case Studies?
- Websites
- Handouts (Trade shows, sales packages, presentations, RFPs, and proposals)
- Media releases
- Brochures
- Newsletters
- ezine articles
- Magazines
- Blogs
- e-mails (eblasts)
- Ads

Trade shows and presentations are all about how much information you can impart while you have the prospect's attention. Don't count on your documents coming out of the trade show bag or binder once your prospects are back at their office. Get your point across right away as they stand by your booth or in the meeting room. Point to the headlines and subheads that outline your story and the photos that complete it. Then get them talking. The name of the game is snagging attention!

Media releases, articles, eblasts, and blog posts: All these avenues provide excellent coverage of your story. Depending on the length of your case study versus the size of the article you wish to use for each medium, you can cut-down your

1: What is a Case Study?

study to a summary and include a quote from your client. Link to the full story on your website or use an opt-in form to build your contact list.

Testimonials: Even with the full case study on your website, a good quote from the customer is still invaluable. Pull the best from your study and use it in sidebars or footers on your site, in brochures, and in blog posts. NOTE: When your customer signs-off on the case study, ask if you may use the quotes for testimonials in other marketing materials. Aside from the legal responsibility of ensuring you've got their permission, the last thing you want to do is strain your professional relationship by overstepping their perceived boundary line.

> **A word on subjects with heavy use of technical information.**
> Before breaking into your industry jargon, think about whether it's a necessary part of the story. What *must* be included for it to make sense? Does your particular readership expect technical or science language? If you peppered-in a few eye-catching details and words and stripped-away the rest for a follow-up report, would a reader be disappointed or intrigued to know more and call? Perhaps instead of a case study, the better vehicle for your detailed information is a white paper.

What Copywriters Know to Give Them an Edge And You Can Learn

Every profession has its tricks of the trade. As you work your way through this book, keep these important points in mind to stay motivated.

- *Planning is the key to every professional piece of writing.* One of my technical writing professors once said planning the content structure can take up to 80% of the time in writing manuals. Time spent coming up with concepts

What Copywriters Know to Give Them an Edge

in marketing and developing the text for a brochure (the smaller the size the harder they are to write well) follow a similar pre-writing schedule. This is where, as a writer, you might find yourself being asked by your boss, "Why is it taking you so long?" Keep your notes and work-up drafts to show the thought process even if you can't account for the thinking and doodling time over lunch, at home, and in the car.

- *You can fix a bad page.* If you remember this, you'll never sit frozen with a blank page/screen in front of you. No one goes to print with their first draft. Once you get a feel for the techniques I show you in the writing and editing section, you'll be able to apply them to all your writing tasks. The case study template is designed to reduce the effort in information gathering and help you to structure your case studies with confidence.
- *When you've finished writing you'll move on to editing.* You may have heard the phrase, "writing is rewriting," but this isn't as bad as it sounds. The fun actually starts once you've put the first draft together, and with a great blueprint, your first draft will be simpler than any business document you've written before. Even so, we'll cover first- and second-pass editing tricks to give your case study a professional polish.
- See chapters 6, 7, & 8 for more on writing and editing.

DO IT!
An easy start. Think of all the ways you could use case studies to promote your business. Keep reading!

2: Choose Your Case Study

Your first case study is often the easiest – *if* you keep it simple. In fact, the first one is often inspired by a particularly interesting or successful implementation or a customer's praise, and it practically writes itself.

As with all case studies, keep your focus on the topic or challenge. Choose one and explore it, choose two at the very most and only if the topics are closely intertwined. Case studies aren't the place to drag out the laundry list of features and benefits. Your customer had one main reason to purchase your product. That's the area you'll showcase.

What do you do about the five other features your widget has?

Go find more happy customers who have purchased your product for each of those reasons! This way you're building a significant case study folder *and* you're getting feedback on a number of popular benefits for just one product. Watch the search engine optimization (SEO) for your website or blog soar as the number of case studies and frequency of updates increase.

2: Choose Your Case Study

Your Readers...Do You Know Who They Are?

Do you sell to business or the consumer? Either way, you're looking for sales, and you've probably got a good idea of your target audience. Your case studies must reflect this in their style.

If you're writing to businesses, you'll be more likely to do the following:
- Use industry terms.
- Show benefits targeted toward bottom lines, growth, or increased output.
- Expect a certain depth of knowledge on the subject from your readers or they most likely wouldn't be searching for a site like yours in the first place.

In doing this, you'll soon notice yourself telling a story that appeals to your business peers.

Case studies work well when you target to the consumer, too. For this group, you might find yourself doing these things:
- Using more detailed explanations (Avoid dumbing-down!) This group wants knowledge to make wise choices, but they don't need all the details of the inner workings.
- Giving more benefits and explaining the WIIFM (what's in it for me?)

Pretend you can see your reader in front of you and talk it out.

Who Will Write Your Case Study?

...and who might *not* be the best person.

Before you appoint your project manager to add case study writing to his tasks, you might be surprised to learn the person with the most knowledge on the subject often isn't the best person to write about it.

Who Will Write Your Case Study?

Sometimes when I sit across from a potential client, he or she is concerned I might not be specialized in their field as a writer. I've got clients in transportation, telecommunications, health care, and a dozen other industries – but perhaps not in the sector they build widgets for. In case study writing, as in most customer-facing documents, this is a bonus. So don't be worried if you've had only a passing introduction to the project and your boss suddenly asks you to write its case study.

Why are non-experts often better for the job? It's for the same reason non-experts are often a better choice to write user guides. Experts quite often miss including critical information readers need. They are so immersed in their high-level work every day, they don't recognize the basics customers need to comprehend the small pieces of logic. These concepts simply aren't on the expert's radar.

When I change hats and am asked to edit product instructions or a report written by a subject matter expert (SME) – I often find leaps in logic and whole blocks of missing information once I've ensured the document is actually structured in the correct sequence. Structure – then content. We'll talk about this more as we go on.

Recognizing a missing link in logic is a much simpler task for someone coming in cold on the project. It's the same in writing as in editing. If you follow-along with the information, and suddenly can't connect the dots, you've found a hole. An expert's eye often jumps the omission the same way we don't see missing words in a sentence. If you're a product expert writing this case study, find someone unrelated to the project and ask them to review each step of your logic as a usability test.

So who *is* the best person to write your company case studies?

2: Choose Your Case Study

Anyone with good language skills – not necessarily trained in writing but someone with a respectable command of the language and a conversational style. A business casual tone is the direction we're heading. I'll cover writing techniques in a later chapter. For now, look for someone who can study the project, do research independently, recognize the challenges and solutions, and have a pleasant manner in interviewing your customer contact and your own project experts.

Someone who won't stress-out or over-analyze the task is a better choice. Stress equals tight, stilted language with a Thesaurus sound to it.

Knowledge of case study writing isn't necessary. All the tools you'll need are in this guide.

Note: After writing a few case studies you'll notice a company tone or style of writing emerge. This is what you'll strive for in all your case studies. Your writers might not stay the same but your company style should.

Finding Clients and Topics

Often the perfect case study opportunity just drops in your lap. Your customer is thrilled, your product runs like a dream, your team was innovative in their installation and customer service efforts, and your customer offered to give you an interview for a case study.

Of course you said, "Yes!" But take a step back before you set up the interview and think about timing. A case study written now would no doubt be filled with glowing remarks and enthusiasm. All good. What it might not have is a large enough interval between the installation and the interview to provide customer metrics on just how great your product is. Then again, if you wait three months the energy has dissipated and pinning-down the customer could be difficult. Neither option is right or wrong. Each project should be analyzed on its own merits. If you have a chance to interview right away – great. You can always ask for numbers when you go back for your six month follow-up. Case studies can be updated!

Before calling the clients you feel most comfortable with – review their projects against the information in the Case Study Template (See chapter 4.) In choosing a topic, you want a balance between a project that was too simple to grab your readers' attention and one so complex that finding a single challenge to discuss might prove difficult or confusing without the context around it.

Getting to Yes

When approaching a client for a case study and even asking to mention their name in a newsletter, I've found these things to be true:

- The bigger the company (more credibility for you if you can snag them), the more difficult it is getting to "yes."
- If the project was complex, you might have more than one case study in hand. Remember the one or two challenges maximum rule? Get the okay to write two studies and combine your questions into one interview. With two cases studies from the same company, you've got instant credibility.
- Sometimes a client offers to give you a case study but the project wasn't all that exciting from your perspective. What do you do? Take it! First, because you can't offend a customer, and second, because all your product solutions *are* exciting! The client came to you with a problem and you solved it. Sometimes what feels like the least

significant product benefit to you means a crisis averted for your client. Remember... it's their story.
- Perhaps your client does say yes, but his schedule never quite jives with yours or your writer's for an interview. Suggest to him you understand he's busy and you'd like to help take the case study off his plate. Suggest he hand the interview over to his project manager or another member of the team. This way you won't lose the opportunity... because there's a good chance the whole issue *will* fold after a third reschedule. Your client still has sign-off rights, so he'll be happy too.

For variety, look to your smaller customers, as well. Show your innovative thinking in helping small businesses with complex problems. You're the good guy! And there are plenty of other small business owners out there surfing for solutions!

CAUTION: When "Yes" Goes Bad

Clients can be tricky when it comes to telling the world about their experience. It's not that your contact suddenly doesn't like your product, she's just been told "no" by her VP. But why?
- Many companies don't want their competitors to know about a cost/time-saving service they've just implemented.
- Often, companies have policies about attaching their name to another company or brand.

Both of these party-stoppers happen frequently enough for you to be aware and proactive in the early stages before investing time in research and writing. Ask your contact if she'd mind checking the idea with her boss or legal department before you begin. If a company is large enough to have a legal department, quite often they are the ones to nix the study. Usually, though, it's a VP being cautious. Either way, your contact saves face by having someone to blame and you haven't spent hours on a document you can't use. And you *cannot* use it without their permission. The best you can do is revise it to hide the customer's and even their business-type's identity.

Research

Research doesn't have to be extensive. The trick is knowing which details to choose to bring the case study alive. If you have good communications throughout your company, likely everyone on staff knows more about your products and services than you realize and you can use this to your advantage.

Prior to interviewing the client, speak with the project manager and any other key people in your company who handled the solution and installation.

By the time you or your writer interviews the client, he or she must have these things:

- A solid understanding of the project from your company's perspective. This includes any problems raised and solved along the way.
- A good feel for the customer's business, products/services, and company culture. The latter is crucial for bringing-out a personal slant readers can identify with.

DO IT!
We have lots to think about in this chapter.
- Which customer projects pop out at you as being great candidates for a case study?
- Who makes up your audience?
- Who will you choose as a writer, if it isn't you?

Go find a *yes* from your customer and start researching!

3: Structure the Case Study

The Case Study and Classic Story Structure

The basic structure of a case study has been around for years.

- (Challenge) A customer has a problem to be explained
- (Approach) Your company has a solution and implementation to be discussed
- (Results) The results are a marvelous win-win for both parties

We can break this structure further into sub-sections, which you'll see as we go through the structure in detail. One or two of these might need only a sentence or two in your case study – but those sentences count to the overall integrity of your argument and bringing the reader from point A (reading about a problem) to point B (calling your company to solve their business challenge.) Each of these sub-sections help guide you through the structure and make sure you've captured all these important parts for a logical flow.

If you follow the information starting on page 30, you'll arrive at a perfectly sound, well-argued case study.

3: Structure the Case Study

The biggest change from case studies of the past has been to make them more engaging. Readers have plenty of other things to do with their time. Your job is to make your story so interesting they'll choose to spend that time reading. We do this through the **tone**.

We want to keep the tone in line with the topic, of course, but a conversational style is most successful with business case studies. They're more easily and quickly consumed and remembered by your reader.

So how do we do it?

- By choosing lighter words. Try *use* instead of *utilize* and *you* instead of *the user* for example.
- By using contractions when a sentence feels stilted.
- By writing down what you would say if the person reading was standing in front of you listening instead.
- By following story structure, not just for the case studies but in your articles as well. I've provided additional thoughts on structure in the article section.

In general, case studies already follow a familiar story structure to most books, magazine articles, and movies. Compare the case study to Tolkien's classic *Lord of the Rings*:

Our good people from Middle Earth (customers) have a **problem** (a nasty ring that, in the wrong hands, could destroy the world.) Off goes their hero Frodo (your contact from their company) to find a solution. After a few adventures they arrive at Rivendell (your company) and happily learn of the **solution** (your product.) But they're not done yet. As they strive to **implement** their solution (by throwing the nasty ring into the fires of Mount Doom), they run into Orcs and all manner of obstructions before **succeeding** (results.)

The Case Study and Classic Story Structure

How is the basic case study structure similar to that of our book? In the book, tension is built as the result of obstacles. Without conflict there is no story. People are just not interested. But give them a struggle and a hard won solution and you've got them hooked. Your case study *should* do that, too!

But wait a moment! Wouldn't your product look better if it leapt off the shelf and solved the problem immediately? In real life, haven't you found your products work that way?

Of course they have! Your product is the Magic Elixir of the quest... the answer to the challenge. Nevertheless, your hero (the customer) only becomes the hero because he found you, and he is the person your readers look up to. Your case study is his story, and as we just learned, conflict creates interest.

Think how you recognize the best qualities of our heroes in a book or movie. We watch them under pressure. They start out looking like regular guys (and gals) so we'll connect with them. They might even stumble until they find the right motivation to act – which could be through a dire circumstance or a friend in need. We root for them! We keep reading even if we know the ending will be satisfying because the story itself engages us. We haven't allowed our hero an easy ride.

Your readers want to read about people just like them who have had a problem, sought-out your company, found the ideal solution, and who are willing to tell others about their experience. Don't worry. You still control how much you want to reveal!

Your case studies will engage the reader because you know four things:

- Time is at a premium for prospective customers so your cases studies are short quick reads.
- You spend time to develop the hook that reels-in your readers.

3: Structure the Case Study

- You talk about the struggles as well as the victories.
- Your story structure is so tightly woven, the reader's focus glides effortlessly from the challenge to the natural step of picking up the phone to call you.

The result is, your readers won't be able to pull their eyes away until they've finished reading – and then they'll take action.

Let's see how this all works!

Act One

The Customer and the Challenge

Case studies can open with either the customer or the challenge to great effect. What's a story without interesting characters? But without a compelling plot also, no one will be interested. When you're gathering your information, consider whether the customer name or the challenge they have is more likely to catch a reader's attention.

The Customer

If a Fortune 500 company, for example, agrees to talk about their experience working with you, write their name in the heading and opening paragraph.

- First we see the big name company (touchstone) – then we see the product.
- In the first paragraph, all we need is sufficient information to know who the company is and a few words about their business. The bigger and more recognizable the company, the less general information you need to supply.

As an example headline:

Giant Motor Company Approves KVP Non-Chip Paint for SUV Line

Act One

In this example, we'd all be familiar with the car manufacturer. Then, to keep your prospective customers hooked, we give them details. Which department of the company placed the purchase from you? Who was the contact? Why did they like your paint over their previous supplier's? It's possible your potential client currently buys from them too.

Smaller clients need a little more help in the description area to make them look sufficiently credible for your potential customer to take notice. Your objective isn't to make them look like multi-nationals when they have one shop on the edge of town. In these cases, you might want to center the reader's attention on what you did to solve their industry-type problem. If Oscar's service garage had trouble with their exhaust system during the winter months, perhaps hundreds of other garages do as well. It's the *industry* we'd point out in the headline.

We'll talk about WIIFM (what's in it for me?) throughout the book, and here's a prime example. Your garage owner prospect reading the case study will translate what you did to help Oscar to what you could do for him. He doesn't care about your company...only what it can do to make his life simpler.

Here's an example: This first paragraph would be from a short case study where you'd like to appeal to the truck manufacturing sector as a target audience.

> Joe's Machinery is a manufacturer of speed inhibitors for the transportation industry. "Since the law for controllers was passed last year, we've been running three shifts and still falling behind," said Tim Smith, Operations Manager for Joe's.

The information on the customer's company you pulled together in your research comes into play here. Now that you've introduced the customer, you'll use what you know about them

3: Structure the Case Study

later in the case study to bring their business and staff to life with only a few details.

The Challenge

But what if wind turbines are in the news lately and your company has just had a breakthrough with noise reduction? You'd use that news hook to your advantage and fill your header and subhead with the challenge, followed by the customer information.

"Silent Running" Wind Turbines Applauded as Noise By-laws are Urged
Community Members are Jubilant as City Installs 10 KVP Turbines Along Residential Side Road

In this case, you're grabbing a news hook of noisy wind turbines and saying how your turbines are different. The city, a big client in itself, and your company's name are played down slightly in favor of snagging the reader's eye.

First we see the news hook – then we see the client.

We'll discuss headlines and subheads in more detail in the writing section. For now, give some thought to the client and your company's role in solving their problem. Which angle will capture your readers' attention as they scan the headings of your case studies?

Just as in a book or movie, we've hooked the readers with a problem they can relate to and given them someone to root for.

> Keep in mind, "Specifics sell." Target one or two challenges at the most. Once you've narrowed the focus to one area, the depth of your solution in detail can be illustrated, yet the case study remains short and succinct.

Act Two

The Solution

The solution part of the case study can be broken into four sections: the Quest, Turning Point, Solution, and Implementation.

The Quest (also known as the Approach)

At this point in your story, your customer exercises his due diligence by researching several potential solutions prior to finding your company. This could include meetings with staff to explore solving the problem themselves or how they tried a competitor's product (not naming names) that didn't work.

You needn't be too lengthy. Ideas the company discussed or tried internally can be mentioned – if you think your readers might consider a similar course of action – but make sure you also explain why they didn't work.

For example, perhaps the customer evaluated the benefits and drawbacks of pneumatic versus hydraulic pumps before making a decision to purchase. Maybe they did a 30-day trial with your competitor's product. As you describe the pros and cons, your reader is drawn into the decision-making process.

IMPORTANT: Don't discuss your product just yet. This section is purely the process toward discovery.

Why do we include this background information?

Readers don't assume your company service was the first solution popping into the mind of your customer. Even if it was, you won't convince your readers of this. By working through alternatives, they see the logical progression while getting a third party nudge in your direction. This is a much more powerful incentive to elicit trust in your company than any amount of marketing could achieve.

3: Structure the Case Study

In fiction, the quest is where the hero gets batted around by the villain. He gets clobbered with setback after setback. We learn more about his character through this diversity and, if he's developed properly, we root for him just as we'll root for your customer.

> Raise the stakes to put the reader behind your customer in his problem. By doing this, readers will identify with your customer and follow him through to his decision in choosing your company.

The Discovery

Rolling-in on the heels of the quest, your customer discovers your company and the solution you're writing about for this case study. This discovery gives you the perfect transition between the quest and solution dialogue, plus it enables you to put your company in a good light.

- Keep this paragraph short but noticeable. It's your company's first appearance on stage!
- Tell readers how the customer found you.
- What made them decide your company was the best for them?
- Mention your company by name if you can.

This small but mighty section is a turning point in your story arc. It's the crisis point that comes half to two-thirds of the way into a book or movie. The hero has outsmarted a few villains and now thinks he has discovered the treasure... or the solution to a problem...or believes he's completed his adventure by securing the pot of gold.

Act Two

The Solution

Although the quest and discovery have been part of the single *approach* category in a traditional case study format, by further breaking this into sections as we have, your task of presenting the information in the proper sequence is much easier. Plus, jumping straight to a solution from the write-up of the company and its problem, with no build-up of the struggles, becomes an emotionless play of events.

> No emotion = reduced impetus to take action
> (and to give you a sale)

By now, to create this tension, you've shown the problem and taken the reader step-by-step toward solving it until they found your company. Your reader is ready for a break.

Here is where, at last, you'll write a paragraph or two on how your solution works.

Be specific to answer the challenge at hand. This is the only thing that matters to your reader right now.

Trying to squeak-in a few other product features will stop the story cold. Your reader will smell the hard sell and you can say good-bye to a sale. **Remember, the vehicle of the case study is your *customer's* story, not yours, even though you relate it.**

Remember the People

In the traditional sense, when we think of a customer, we think of a person – not bricks and mortar or a brand name. Yet it's easy to lose sight of this when we're solving problems or writing reports.

Include information on the people from both companies when discussing your winning solution. Add quotes. Add the setting. You'll bring life to the story and, through it, the reader can't help but envision her own staff in the same situation.

3: Structure the Case Study

IMPORTANT:
- Keep the sales pitch until the end of the case study or for specific sales letters. Don't spoil your story now!
- Keep the customer's problem and *how your solution solved it* firmly in mind.
- Use specific details to bring the setting to life and draw focus. See the writing chapter for more on writing specifics!

Pitch your product... but show how it solves the problem and keep the customers' mantra in mind. "What's in it for me?" They should feel a sense of closure.

The installation or implementation of the solution

We're not done yet. The customer has chosen your product – but what now? Your readers want to know! You have them on the hook...don't let them off! You'll not only ruin a perfectly good story but you'll lose their interest as well.

Right about now your mind (and maybe your boss) is screaming at you to, "Start writing already! The customer plugged-in our widget and watched their return on investment (ROI) skyrocket. What's not to like?"

Unfortunately, this is exactly the wrong approach. Who wants to see Sherlock Holmes succeed without a struggle with Moriarty? The more equally matched the villain, the better the story. **The more challenging the problem, the better your solution will look. It's the law of relativity.**

From a credibility standpoint, readers expect a few bumps in any implementation and will be skeptical of a too-simple turnkey solution. Hopefully your installation really *did* go smoothly, but to keep the reader's interest, the more tension the better.

Act Two

You keep the integrity of your company strong when you open with good points, follow with any difficulties (NOTE: Not a malfunctioning product!), and end with how the teams worked through the steps in an innovative way. Again here, you don't need to dwell on issues, but *do* include them. If the project had such a disaster that it's hard to overlook, it probably isn't a good contender for a case study anyway.

NOTE: What happens if everything went right! (Which is most of the time, of course!) Try turning the tension in the story over to the customer's challenge. *"Even though we remained ahead of schedule, Joe's client suddenly moved their deadline forward by two weeks. With help from Joe's senior mechanic, we were able to install the stage-one widget-maker first, on one side of the floor. This gave their line crew the opportunity to increase their parts inventory while we continued installing the major manufacturing equipment."* Here, the reader gets his tense moment yet your company looks innovative as well as cognizant of your client's ongoing business during the project.

Let's review the importance of being specific. Compare the quote above to this: *"The customer's client unexpectedly brought their deadline forward two weeks leading us to quick action to enable Joe's to continue manufacturing while we worked in another area of the plant."* No contest. Yet when we write in a hurry, this latter non-specific version is our usual output. Notice how we can't visualize people in the second version and how the intensity drops because of it?

3: Structure the Case Study

Act Three

The Results

With the hero safely home after saving the world, everyone sits around for a few moments to rehash what happened. This ties up loose ends and gives the reader or movie viewer a chance to unwind. For a book author, a good ending sells the next book and a poor one loses the reader.

As a case study writer, you've spun a tale with emotional highs and lows, good characters, and a realistic view of the events as they happened. Now you must equally wrap the story to lead the reader toward considering your company for their next project, or they'll just click to the next page that takes their interest. Here is where you sell, and yet because it's part of *your customer's reflection* on the project, you're technically not advertising yourself, your customer is. Through this, you have instant credibility from this third party.

In the result's section, we tell the world how the customer now uses your product or service, and we touch as many specifics as we can for the reader to identify with.

- **Show the benefits.** More than a shopping list from your sales brochure, these benefits need to target the challenge they solved and, where possible, show statistics or a favorably increased bottom line.
- **Tell about any unforeseen bonus benefits.** Perhaps the workflow was more streamlined and staff didn't have to stay late at month end any longer. Be as specific as you can to connect with your reader without getting wordy. Saying the workflow was better or more streamlined is just another sales line...but saying the staff didn't have to stay late any longer and you've suddenly brought immediacy and humanity to the benefit.

Act Three

- **How well did the staff accept the new product or service?** Were they impressed by the installation? In other words, did it affect them in their daily routine? Unhappy or hampered staff means lower morale and possibly lower production. Providing the employee-take on the project is a huge area to explore. Capitalize on it if you can.
- **What cost savings have there been and in what areas?** This isn't your company to demand numbers from, but if your contact is willing, he might give percentages over the previous year. This doesn't divulge too much at their end but speaks highly of your company's success.

If you've given them enough time to build a trend, say two or three months, they've had the opportunity to collect the numbers on their return on investment. Here again you could ask for an ROI percentage increase.

To recap: As best as possible, substantiate every claim you relate. If the production rate increased – tell us by what percent. If you say manufacturing costs dropped – explain in what area of the company and by how much. **Without results, you've got no case study.** Your customer should know that going in. If the hard numbers or percentages are too few, try for the personal and emotional benefits which should be included anyway.

DO IT!
Consider if your customer name or the challenge should go in lead position. Once you've chosen this, write down the major points of the project from your perspective. Include what you feel the customer's challenge was, how your company customized your solution for them, and what might be considered a tension point in the implementation – without drawing negative attention to your company or product.

4: The Template

Introduction to the Case Study Template

Before going further and setting-up your client interview, let's have a look at the template you'll be using.

Everything I've discussed about structure is built into the Case Study template you'll find here. I designed this to help guide you through the data gathering and writing process yet enable you to customize your case study quickly and easily within the structure without restricting the questions you ask.

The importance of the template is the structure you'll follow. By dividing the document into the story structure divisions, you are better able to sense where each chunk of information goes and how it keeps the writing task manageable and less intimidating.

We can usually face writing a few paragraphs without too much apprehension, and this organization of writing one section at a time is set up for exactly that style of approach. Logic flows naturally when you stick with the structure of the template.

4: The Template

Case Study Template

Use this template as a basis for your interview questions and to develop your case study structure.

- Add and subtract information to suit your individual requirements.
- Move data around as long as the logic flows within each section and into the one following.
- Keep the main headings in the same generally accepted order:

1 & 2	Challenge or Customer goes in first position followed by the other
3	Solution – including the quest (approach) / discovery (turning point) / solution
4	Implementation of the solution
5	Results

To keep on message and remember all the necessary parts, think of your case study as one cohesive story cobbled together by chapters or scenes.

Customer information

- Company name:
- Contact name:
- Direct phone line or cell:
- e-mail address:
- Website URL:
- Other

Case Study Template

Background information on the project

Enter as little or as much as you wish. This could include relevant points you might or might not use in the case study but which were integral to the project such as a limited time frame, budgets, a specific goal, a particular audience group or other restrictions that limited your choices of solution.

The Customer – If the customer's name or industry will catch your readers' attention – lead with this section.

Briefly describe the customer's business. (Fill this in as much as you can ahead of time using your research. As you speak with the client, include one or two specifics that might be of interest to your readers.)

- What does the company do?
- What is its main industry sector?
- What is it recognized for? (Look for a hook the reader would find interesting.)
- What division or department was affected by this project?
- Other points of interest.

The Challenge – If the challenge the customer faced will be more interesting to your readers – lead with this section. You'll focus on one (if possible) or two (maximum) central issues for this case study.

- What were the conditions or challenges you faced before using our product or service?
- (As applicable) From these, what one or two challenges were most significant? We'd like to narrow the focus

4: The Template

for this study. (These should correspond to the solution you'll want to write about.)
- What would have been the consequences if you could not find a solution to this condition?
- Additional details.

The Solution

The Quest (Approach)

- Explain what steps you took in-house prior to looking for a solution outside your company?
- What other products or solutions did you consider before coming to us? (Competitor products and company names will not be mentioned in the study.)
- What reasons turned you off using these products or services? (Example – too complex to use, inability to customize, didn't solve problem, too costly.)
- Additional details.

Note: This is part of the discovery process. Do not discuss your product yet.

Turning point/Discovery (Now we introduce your company. Keep this to two or three sentences.)
- How did you find our company?
- What was it about our company or product that led you to choose us? (Unearth one or two specifics if possible. This is a crucial selling point.)
- Additional details.

Case Study Template

The Solution

- Pre-fill this section with a paragraph or two on your company's thought processes and steps to providing an innovative solution.
- During the interview with your client, ask for his recollection of the process. The similarities and differences in recollection can be eye-opening!
- Be specific. Remember you are trying to sell this product, so explaining why it would work to solve the client's challenge should go here.
- Additional details.

Implementing the solution

- How long ago was the implementation?
- How would you describe the implementation process over all?
- Was there down time for your company?
- How did this affect your staff or production?
- What challenges surfaced for you (the customer)?
- What challenges did the implementation team run into?
- How did the team handle these challenges?
- Do you feel they went the extra mile to assist you?
- Additional details.

Results

- Did this solution solve most or all of your original challenge?
- How well is the product/solution still meeting or surpassing your expectations?
- Was there an unexpected added value in the solution? For example, did you find other parts of your business or work-flow ran better as a result of the implementation?

4: The Template

- Would you share specifics with us in either a dollar value or percentage, such as production increases, sales increases, staff-related issues, or ROI?
- Over what time period did you see this happening?
- Would you recommend our company to others?

Closing (IMPORTANT!)

Rework these questions to casually include them in your closing statements.

- May I contact you again if I need clarification?
- Should I speak with anyone else in your company for details on points we covered? (The client may ask you to speak with one of his staff earlier in the conversation.)
- Did you have a chance to try (named) feature as well? (If your contact hasn't shown signs of terminating the call, draw feedback on other features for your media release or blog.)
- Is there anything else you would like to say about this project, our company, or our people? (Often your best quotes come from these last words as long as the person doesn't feel as though that's what you're after!)

Visit **www.learnit-doit.com/cstemp10.html**
for a printable copy of the template and
10 Tips to Strengthening Your Writing

DO IT!
Jot down these structural headings on a sheet of paper, copy the template, or visit our website for a downloadable copy and list your recollections of the project (Point form – See page 58!) Once you've spoken with your customer, you'll be able to see how your thoughts mesh or differ from theirs and you're on your way to an interesting exploration of the truth behind your project.

5: The Customer Interview

Why do we need a customer interview?

"Can't I wing it?" you ask. I mean, who knows your products and services better than you do, right?

Sorry. As much as I'd love to say the customer interview is unnecessary – the case study *is* their story and only they know the side your readers want to see. You can technically write one without the customer's help, but what's the point? You need their sign-off before you can use it anyway, so why not get the detailed information only they can provide, right at the start?

Here are your focal points for the interview, which you will find in the template:

- What was the customer's challenge?
- Who else's product/service (if any) did they investigate?
- Why did they choose your product/service?
- How well is the product/service still meeting or surpassing their expectations?

This information, coming from the customer, brings credibility to your case study, and without that you have no testimonial.

5: The Customer Interview

Customer Sign-Off

This leads us to a critical, no exceptions step required for every case study, whether you've interviewed the customer or not. If you aren't given a sign-off by your customer, **do not** mention their company and certainly refrain from using any form of quote, direct or paraphrased, collected from past casual conversations. **The customer must give their okay before you can publish the study. No exceptions.** I'd recommend you get that in writing as well.

What could happen if you ignore this?
At worst, the customer could take legal action. If you've reported anything not true or made up your own quotes without approval, libel charges could be laid. They could also accuse you and your company of publishing confidential or proprietary information for the competition to read.

Almost as bad, they might pull their business from you or relations could become strained and, poof...no more business or referrals.

I've seen this happen with newsletters as well, another vehicle where my clients like to discuss their successes and where their customers often prefer not to let the competition know. One company disregarded my recommendation to request permission to talk about a project. They took considerable criticism from their customer to the effect of needless loss of good will between them afterwards. Another client always considers their customers first and works within their comfort zone. Because of this, they have plenty of testimonials to their credit.

This little show stopper of signing-off has been the reason many case studies become anonymous in nature, describing similar projects for fabricated companies. It's a vexing situation, and the case study loses power.

Preparation

You've had a look at the template and no doubt have plenty of specific questions to add to it. Go ahead and write them down for the interview. You might not need all the information you gather, but you'll have a firmer base for your materials.

> **Information for Other Materials**
>
> Keep other marketing materials in mind as you formulate your questions.
>
> What other information could you use for a media release? An article? A series of blog posts or an eblast?

If you've been tossing around the idea of doing a case study, but haven't yet approached the customer, ask now before you put another minute of work into it. You have a terrific excuse to call just by following-up on your sale or installation. If they're still ecstatic – ask if they'd be willing to share their thoughts for a case study (you will write for them.) If they've had problems – you've got your work cut out for you in keeping them happy. Move on to the next customer on your list for the case study.

Keep these points in mind for your initial approach:

- Ensure your contact has the seniority to say yes. As we discussed in "Getting to Yes," you don't want to put all the work into your study only to have the VP say no.
- Tell your contact you can send a list of questions a day or two in advance so he can prepare.
- Offer him the opportunity to include points not included in the questions. If his points don't mesh with your study, use them in another vehicle and get sign-off for it along with the case study.
- Write questions pertinent to the challenge of the case study and any other materials you wish to cover in the same interview. Keep your focus!

5: The Customer Interview

- Do your research! The only way you can ask intelligent questions is to be prepared.
- In setting up the interview time, check you have the correct number to call, and tell your contact *you* will place the call. Also allow for the possibility of last minute meetings at their side and let him know this isn't a problem. (You've got all the time in the world, right? He's your customer!)

Making the Interview Call

NOTE: For those who feel confident in interviewing, you might wish to skip this section.

But if the task of conducting a phone interview has been passed along to you, and you're terrified at the thought, you're among good company. The first interview I conducted was for a newsletter article and it was set for nine in the morning. My contact didn't answer when I called. The company is quite large and I knew the unexpected happens in business so, nerves aside, I waited. A half-hour later I politely tried again and got the same voice mail. Some time later, I received an apologetic e-mail asking if we could speak after hours, say, at five-thirty.

Five-thirty came and went with another voice mail and my nerves were now ragged. By six o'clock my husband brought me a couple of pieces of fried chicken and a glass of Pinot Grigio as I clung to the phone in the office. I don't remember eating the chicken, but half-way through the wine I realized my head was getting light (probably from missing lunch and more than nine hours of nerves building.)

Then the phone rang.

Did I mention I hadn't yet bought a digital recorder to hook into the phone?

Making the Interview Call

And yet, the interview went well, as have the hundreds I've done since. If I can do it with this prestigious start, so can you.

Here are a few tricks to help:
- **Smile.** It shows up in your voice and makes you feel better. Truly. The trick is to remember.
- **Breathe.** When we're nervous we shallow-breathe. Take two deep breaths in through the nose and out through the mouth and imagine the nerves flowing out with it.
- **Realize most case studies are only 500 – 800 words long.** That might sound like a lot, but 500 words fits a letter page with one or two small photos. With all the sections you have to cover (already outlined in your template), you'll find yourself cutting half of what you've gathered!
- **Relax.** You've done your research. You'll be amazed at how much information you can add on your own.
- **Record the interview.** Let your interviewee know. It's the law in many places and courteous in general. If they hesitate, I usually explain I use it so I won't inadvertently misquote anything they have to say. Take notes anyway. Recorders come with Gremlins.
- **Go for specifics** when the customer starts to generalize. Here's an example from the Results section of a case study:

Customer:	It didn't take long to see results after you installed the widget for us.
You:	Within a few days would you say?
Customer:	Definitely.
You:	And what kind of results did you have?
Customer:	Our first weekly report showed a one-third increase in production.

    Notice the difference?

5: The Customer Interview

- **Open with one or two pleasantries** and get on with the job. Don't waste your contact's time.
- **Listen well.** Your customer might have taken the time to write everything down and is just as anxious to get this done as you are. If he wants to talk, and he's kept on topic, let him! Follow his lead and only interject if you don't understand a point. Check off the areas in the template as he touches on them. There's no need to go in order. Then circle back to anything omitted when he's finished.

Find the personal perspective

The human element of a project can get lost as you're writing about it, but people are affected in any new service or equipment installation. If the staff at your customer's company found the installation gave minimal disruption (or they actually enjoyed involving themselves in the process) then maybe your prospective customer's staff would too. Make sure you put this in your case study. Ask your customer about staff involvement and reaction during the quest, implementation, and results stages to give your case study life and provide a setting for future customers to envision.

DO ask for the *cons* as well as the *pros*. As I spoke about earlier, discussing the challenges illuminates how well your company took care of them.

Numbers sell

Look for opportunities to nudge the contact for approximate increases in productivity or percentages in the ROI or cost savings since they've used the product. Substantiate your claims. "Did you find the insulation saved heating costs as well? Could you give me an approximate percentage over this time last year?"

Making the Interview Call

Ending the call

In closing the call, ensure you capture how well your product has solved the challenge you discussed up front. This takes the case study full circle and tends to bring the interview back to a conversational tone. You'll often hear the sigh of relief at the other end (to mask your own.) It's an off-the-record feel.

This is a great time to ask what your contact thought of one or two other product features. "By the way, did you have a chance to try the delayed-sync function yet?" Just one little quote on this function gives you variety for your other marketing pieces!

> **Using Recording Equipment**
>
> Always record your interviews. Not only does this enable you to capture accurate information, but you've got proof the client gave it to you freely.
>
> Look for two things when buying a recorder:
> - The ability to hook it up to your phone.
> - The ability to download the interview to your computer. The interview then becomes part of your client's file.

NOTE: Always respect confidentiality! If the client gives you background or an anecdote to help you understand an idea – but says "you don't have to print this" it means *don't print this.* You're not writing an exposé.

Before you disconnect... **Always, always, always ask, "Is there anything you'd like to add before we close?"** Some of the best quotes come from these last few words because the customer, if he does take advantage of this, will often
- Give you a fabulous recap statement or,
- Expound on what great people you have at your company or,

5: The Customer Interview

- Suddenly tell you an anecdote with the most perfect examples of what the new product has done for them.

Take advantage of this wonderful opportunity.

Now...
Smile – Breathe – Dial

The Transcript

After your call, download the recording to your computer immediately. Even if you can't take the time to transcribe it just yet, you'll have a safe copy to work from when you're ready. Digital recordings are easily erased.

In the early days, I worked exhaustively on getting every word typed exactly as spoken. This can soon double the length of the interview time itself if you stop and start the recording as often as I do in transcribing!

You want to strive for accuracy, but you'll notice moments in the conversation where your contact gives you a little background, or even tells you something off the record. Generally I recap this background information because it helps me understand the reasons behind their decisions or processes. I don't type-up off-the-record information. I don't want to inadvertently use a fact told to me in confidence. This isn't investigative journalism. It's a case study. You want to keep your customer happy with you. When you're picking a chunk of information from the interview later on, it's easy to miss the words, "in confidence" a line or two above it. Stay safe and leave it out of the transcript.

Watch for any opportunity to pull a quote from the conversation. Sometimes a few kind words about your company

The Recording

or staff can be worked into a larger quote. Dialog that mentions cost and time savings or increased production are perfect. If the words sound like a quote – they probably are. Highlight them for the case study or a future testimonial.

The Recording

Keep your digital recordings for further reference if required. I usually save them in the same folder in the computer as the case study. This way anyone doing a search later can easily find the notes, recording, and copy of the case study in a logical spot even if you have a separate file for all the company's published case studies too.

In the next chapter I'll help you develop potential quotes into eye-catchers for your readers.

DO IT!
Time to dip your toe in the water!
- Prepare your questions pertinent to the case study.
- Make a copy of the interview template.
- Sharpen your pencil and turn on your recorder.

Have fun!

6: Prepare to Write

The template is a powerful tool for gathering and arranging all the information you'll need for a standard case study structure.

To prepare for writing, you'll now flow all the necessary information from your interview and research into the final case study template.

Highlight the Important Information

Start with a fresh template if you've already used one for your interview notes.

- Begin by writing down points from your interview and your research for each question on the template. It's important you use point form and NOT full sentences. I'll explain why in a moment.

- Next, highlight passages in your transcript that look like quotes plus words or phrases you'd like to see in a quote – even if it's incomplete.

6: Prepare to Write

Why We Use Point Form

Even seasoned writers fall victim to the *territorial instinct*. New writers are much more at risk of becoming immobilized by it. I'm talking about the near obsession to holding onto our words once they've been written down. Here's a trick to help you to avoid the problem in the first place. Use point form instead of sentences during the early stages of your draft.

Try this quick experiment and see how the concept works (Do each step first before reading the next one!):
  Step 1: Using point form only, list three reasons why you'd like to go to Hawaii for your next vacation... or why you'd prefer to go skiing.
  Step 2: Now write them again as three *full sentences.*
  Step 3: Did I say three things? I meant to say two! Go back and cut one of your three things from each of the above lists.

Did you notice a hesitation in deleting the full sentence from the step two list? Deleting a point is much simpler. When cutting information, it's easier to chop an idea in point form before you've worked on it, crafted it, and sent it out into the world as a sentence.

We as writers tend to *own* our sentences but we have almost no loyalty to a bullet point. This is important when gathering information and outlining because we invariably end up with too much. It's easier to see the main thought in points – and also easier to recognize when that point might not belong in a paragraph – chapter – or book. Plus bullet points sometimes need to stay just as they are for the reader to see quickly.

Professional writers routinely cut scenes and whole chapters from first, second, or third drafts when they realize the topic doesn't *stick to the goal* of the book. They've learned how *not* to own the words they write. It's still a little punch in the gut to cut a favorite line or paragraph, but looking at the passage as words – just words – helps. This starts by learning how to throw away your points.

Use Quotations

Put the main information from your transcript into point form

For short case studies, you might find two to four points are as much as you'll need to complete each question. If you need more, you probably have a large enough concept that it needs breaking into subsections.

Think about the flow of your document within each section, and re-order your points to move with the logic allowing for a transition between thoughts when necessary. Mark points for deletion if they don't follow your story thread. The question is, "If I take this point out, will we be missing a piece of vital information to help the prospect make a decision to our favor?" If yes, keep it. If no, consider setting it aside. You could still use it in a collateral document such as a media release, an article, or an eblast.

Incorporating your research

Much to the surprise of new writers, you won't use most of the research you've dug up. And because you've familiarized yourself with the background, you'll be better equipped to ask relevant questions in the interview and, conversely, recognize where not to concentrate. You'll also find your writing is richer because you have that background behind you. For the documents at hand, choose only the points that align with your message.

Use Quotations

Now that you've got the knack of choosing the choicest information, let's raise the hackles of all the journalists out there and talk about quotations, shall we? (Don't worry. We're all after a correct quote – we just have a couple of differences in the way we achieve this.)

6: Prepare to Write

When quoting speakers, our job is to capture their message and respect the intent they gave it in. This means we don't infuse our own point of view (POV) or change an integral piece of content to put the quote in the wrong context. Even so, in business writing we have a few tricks that enable us to keep everyone happy without sticking to the word-for-word accuracy reporters are bound to. Here's where newspaper journalism and business writing part ways – a little.

Respected journalists take great pains to capture quotes word-for-word. In the hundreds of business and marketing documents I've written, only a handful of times has the interviewee asked me to use a quote exactly as he's said it. Instead, one of the first things I hear is, "Try to make me sound good."

Another thing to consider is, in a short case study or article, only two or three quotes will fit, but the content we want to use is distributed over the course of the interview.

We can handle quotations a few ways:

- Include them exactly as they are. Especially in a news-oriented report or when a quote could be misinterpreted, use a full quote within its context to ensure the person's words remain intact. You've kept your recording, right?

- Divide a lengthy quote. Sometimes part of a quote will fit perfectly in the Challenge section of your case study while the another part is relevant only to the Results section or a different marketing piece entirely. Splitting the quote could give you the greatest impact because each powerful part can be used in the right spot.

- Most often, we take what we can from a quote and add bits and pieces of information from the general conversation to fabricate the rest. The tricky part is looking through the

Use Quotations

eyes of your customer. What might she say? How would she phrase that quote? And most importantly, how can I put my customer and her company in the best possible light? The answer? Do the best you can and send it off for approval.

I generally tack on a little note to say, "Make it your own." This way the client knows she can adjust the wording, add to it, and delete from it... but it also serves to say, "Here is the idea for the message I'd like for this spot. How can you make it better for us?"

If they come up with something totally different that no longer works there logically, find or create a place where it will work if you can. Then rewrite the original paragraph quote-free. But if the client's revised quote won't work at all, don't use it. It's still your company's case study to write.

Customers are usually grateful when you take-on the task of writing quotes for them. You prepare the groundwork, make them look good, and if they make a change, it almost always strengthens the content and infuses it with a touch of their personality. And that makes all the difference.

Journalists vs. Business Writers On Quotations

With the case study and any other business materials where you'll write on behalf of your customer, quotations must have sign-off. This gives the customer a chance to correct errors, and add or delete content.

Newspapers are different. Journalists report the news as truthfully as possible and they normally do not show the interviewee the article before it's in print. Being accurate with quotes and having the backup recording to prove them, therefore, is critical.

6: Prepare to Write

Cobbling together a quotation

Let's say your customer gives you a quote on how wonderfully your portal software works for remotely adjusting the temperature of their freezers at 10 locations. Earlier as he chatted with you, he might have mentioned, "If the alarm function hadn't been activated the other day, the back door to that location would have been open all night. Could you imagine what might have happened if someone walked in?"

This statement alone wouldn't work for a quote to show-off your alarm because a door left ajar after hours makes the customer look inept. Still, the information could be re-worked to say, "We purchased the portal software to keep temperature adjustments within our control but, as a bonus, the door alarm system activated last week, alerting us to a potential problem." (The problem was the employee who didn't lock-up, but that's another issue!)

In this example, I took information about the bonus benefit of the alarm for that customer and added it with a comment he'd made earlier about why he chose the software. I've now got two important pieces of information in one, still correct, quote.

Yes...you're telling me I'm being unspecific by not saying what the "potential problem" was, as I've been badgering you to do, and the sentence is weaker because of it. You would be right. Here, I weighed the pros and cons and decided I liked having the quote nonetheless because it touched on an unexpected benefit the customer wanted to mention. How would you handle this? The choice is always yours.

Make Every Word Count

This is a critical point to grasp in writing and why I stress it so often in this book. We were programmed in school to submit stories by word count. Sometimes this meant padding the content to fill out the required number of words.

It's a great exercise for forcing students to keep a pen in hand, but most of us weren't taught the next steps to strong writing unless we took courses in university.

Content must be properly gathered, culled, and structured. Nouns and verbs must be chosen with care. Every word must count toward moving your story, article, or case study to its conclusion. If a paragraph or even one adjective doesn't add value...out it comes!

Will you have to dig deeper to come up with the best wording? Absolutely. But your case study will be a faster read, and packed with great information because of it.

Watch how using specifics, not overuse of adjectives and adverbs, can give even one sentence sales power.

Non-specific and padded:
- "By using this new software, our computer systems helped the agents save a considerable amount of time and respond faster over the course of a day."

Specific...no padding, yet stronger and more memorable:
- "By using KVP's SortRight software, our systems separated the general enquiries from the ones requiring prompt action by our CSRs increasing our response time by 40%."

Using specifics doesn't necessarily make an impact on the number of words you'll end up with on the page – but it does ensure each word brings your most important points to the reader.

6: Prepare to Write

Tighten Your Writing

To reduce the amount of time needed for editing and arrive at a lean document, professional writers do their utmost to leave out the words they'll have to cut later anyway. Sounds simple enough, right?

You might feel the opposite is true – that you'll gladly take any words at all to fill the page. The reality is, once you start, you'll quickly notice the pages keep filling until you're hopelessly beyond your planned word count. This often happens in the early sections when we're worried we don't have sufficient information to see us through.

Sometimes it's the result of not knowing how to explain a point well the first time so we reiterate.

We over-explain or *pad* the document with words that don't add to our message, such as adjectives, adverbs, or redundant explanations.

Until you get the feel of tightening as you write, don't worry about it. Do the best you can and stick with your message. When you've explained the topic you're on, stop writing and go to the next. When you've finished the whole case study, you'll go back to the top and do your first edit. That's when you'll play with the sentences. We'll get to this in the editing section. For now – keep writing and know you'll have a chance to polish later.

Use All the Senses

Keep your audience on the hook by appealing to their emotions. This is marketing. You've added specifics to intrigue their logical business side, which is vital in getting a sale. Appealing to their emotions will guide them to connect with the customer in the case study, who is the hero of the story – the one who gives it

Use All the Senses

credibility – which also leads to a sale. We do this through the five senses. You're writing a story, not a report. Stories succeed when you assist the reader in experiencing them.

We've talked about mentioning the customer's staff to add personality and humanity to the company and its challenge. Watch for places where you can also increase visuals or a tactile experience. Even one or two subtly placed words guides the reader to feel the experience. Watch how this works:

> **Think about a wind turbine with four feathered wings instead of blades.**

Go on, tell me you didn't just try to picture this. It's impossible not to. Our mind is hard-wired this way. Put a visual in front of someone and they have to think it!

Make your reader think of a sight, a sound, a smell that creates a good memory and you'll elicit an emotion.

Let's say your company manufactures food containers with a flip lid that stays with the base. Your client is a bakery who bought these sandwich boxes for their summer giveaway promotion. They chose your product because you wrote this in your marketing material:

> "We developed our individual FlipLid containers after our senior exec, Sally, brought her children to the beach last year and had an incident. She was laying out the sandwiches on paper plates when her three-year-old took-off after a beach ball. Once Sally got everyone back and settled, she finally relaxed with her own chicken salad sandwich. All ready for a mouth-watering bite, she crunched her teeth down on several grains of sand that had blown into the filling..."

I get shivers in my teeth just thinking about it! Almost any pitch the company gives me now will be fair game for a sale!

6: Prepare to Write

You can use this effect to your company's benefit if you plan it well in your case study and any other marketing materials. Make the reader part of your story and not a spectator by including the senses along with people involved in the action.

One Last Check of Your Audience

Now that you've gathered all your information into one spot, you've researched your customer's viewpoint and your own company's, and you're ready to write – think one more time about *who* you're writing for. Picture one or two people specifically if you can and imagine yourself speaking to them. By seeing specific audience members your mind can kick into gear and you'll have no problem choosing the correct language style to use.

DO IT!
You're ready to write. If you've followed along, you've highlighted possible quotations in the transcript, and you've chunked the main points for each topic into your case study template. You know your message and you know where to pump up the visuals, sounds, or tactile components of your story.

You're set to get started!

7: Write the Case Study

You have your template and your points listed in order, so you're ready to write. You can start with the body text or create your title and subhead first. Each of us has our own preference. Go with what feels right to you. If you know your main purpose of the study you might try writing the headline to encapsulate it, otherwise, write the study and create the headline later.

When you get to the body text, your completed template kicks-in. Start at the beginning or at any point that feels comfortable. The modular format of the template lets you work in sections. Later you will check for flow and add transitions as necessary.

Writing the First Words

If you find those first words won't leave your pen or keyboard, try talking them out. What would you say if you were asked about the project? Use your natural voice and language to get started. The style will be much more pleasant and conversational than if you over-think looking for the *good* words.

As you consider the content for the section you're writing, what thoughts come to mind? Jot down two or three main words you want to cover in that opening paragraph – you can gather them

7: Write the Case Study

from the points you wrote down in your outline. For instance, in the side-bar on page 58 where I wrote about using point form, I wasn't sure where to start even though I had my outline in front of me. I chose three words for ideas I knew I wanted covered - *territorial, new writers* (technically two words!), and *trick* and focused only on those. In my outline, I'd written that I wanted to discuss an issue we all face but that I've got a little trick to help you around it. Once I had those three main points, I put them into two rather long opening sentences which I edited later. Go ahead and try it: Choose two or three words and write them into your first sentences. You can always change them later.

Headlines and Subheads

Think of the last time you opened a book or magazine to find two or three mammoth paragraphs staring back. Unless the information was something you really needed to know, you might have turned to another article. Now visualize a magazine page with sidebars and callouts and dialog running here and there throughout the columns. Dialog provides plenty of white space and peps-up your prose with a fast entertaining read.

Headlines and subheads also give the eye relief and provide the reader with a road-map to your document as well.

Skimmers might like to zero-in on the results or the tail end of the solutions section. With a subhead to let them know where

> **Beware the "Clever" Subhead**
>
> Descriptive headlines can feel *oh so boring* sometimes and, as we write, our witty little mind might come up with a snappy headline to draw attention. Use them with caution. The headings are the first thing your readers will see. Give them words they can tie into the project. They'll reward you by continuing to read.

Headlines and Subheads

they are, they can quickly locate the issues (which they hope reflect their own) and read how you overcame them (which you hope will lead to a sales call.)

Just seconds after picking up your case study, your readers can cut to the heart of what *they* want to see, if you show them the way. Headings do that for you.

Traditional or descriptive headlines – Which will you use?
The Challenge – Approach – Results heading format has been so ingrained in us for case studies that many companies don't want to stray from it for fear their case study won't be taken seriously. These headings tell us what to expect in the general story structure, but nothing about this story – your story. Here is where unique titles come into play.

Subheads that capture exactly what the section is about can be skimmed to give the reader a snapshot view of the case study. Just by skimming, the reader knows what the challenges are, who was involved, what was done, and how successful it was. All this can be achieved through the subheads, *if* the writer did a good job recapping what the text is about.

With a sprinkle of keywords here and there, you'll be raising your page level in the search engines as well. (See page 126)

Happily for you, many companies have not yet embraced keywords. So if your competitors are in that group, you're even further ahead.

Here is an example of a subheading that describes the story. Rather than say *Approach* as a typical subhead, a company selling a service that enables customers to control the temperature of off-site buildings might say this:

Remote Control Access Provides Complete Solution

7: Write the Case Study

Read through your subheads when you're finished the case study. If you can pick up the problem and solution from them alone, your work is done!

Write a Masterful Headline

Headlines hook your reader – subheads reel them into the body text. You'll use this skill for your case studies, media releases, articles, and advertising, so spend time discovering what it is about your document that readers want to know. *Hint:* It's not always the message you feel is most important. We've talked about the WIIFM (What's in it for me?) factor in marketing. Nowhere is it more important than in your headlines and subheads to engage your readers with what fascinates *them* and moves them to act.

The following tips will get you started on the intriguing craft of headline writing. Note that some of these styles won't be your best choice for a case study but would work perfectly for an article, media release, or blog post.

For more marketing tips on headlines and ad copy – watch for my LEARN IT - DO IT! book, *Write Your Own Advertising & Marketing Copy.*

- The number one rule always and for everything you write: **Appeal to what the reader wants.** WIIFM – This starts in the headline and goes right through the document.

- **Tell us what your topic is about**. If you're promoting your company's new software portal, put it into the headline or subhead. You might think this is obvious but you'll be surprised at how many times this rule is broken. Flip through your favorite magazine or newspaper and you'll ask yourself what the writer was thinking sometimes. Too

Write a Masterful Headline

much energy is often spent on trying to be clever – but if readers don't know what you'll be discussing right away, they'll move on to something else.

"KVP Acquires Acme Industries" is perfect if both companies are household names and it gives you a news hook. For a small company like KVP, in this case, the service and not the purchased company itself acts as the hook for customers. Try, "KVP Offers Dye-Sublimation Services." Keep it short so the font can be larger. Then explain in the sub-head. "Acquisition of Acme Printing Enables Full Studio Services From Graphic Design Through Commercial Printing."

- **Be honest.** If you hook the reader with hype and let them down, you've lost that person forever.
- **Offer to give free information.** "The 10 Best Ways to Keep Your Network Secure!"
- **Use a top ten list.** These are always eye stoppers and great for ezine articles or advertorials. Something about a top ten list gives readers the feeling they can skip the grunt work and make their life simpler in ten easy steps.
- **Ask a question.** Engage curiosity – but take it a step further. With so much information vying for your reader's attention, an ad headline that asks, "Would You Like to Increase Your Company's Marketing Reach?" might be followed by a, "No thanks." The reader now expects a sales pitch to follow and turns the page – or just can't be bothered to see what you're offering.

7: Write the Case Study

Instead, work your question into a news hook or WIIFM statement. Appeal to the readers' underlying basic need, and if possible, entice them with free information. "Would Your Company Benefit From Free Global Advertising?" Follow this with a prominent subhead, "Try These Five Easy Steps to Social Marketing to Get You Started." Here you've given away just enough to let them try your services on their own and to find out maybe they could use your help to build a proper social media plan for them.

- **Use positive wording.** Once in a while we'll use a negative in a title or text for emphasis or clarity. "Don't turn off the anti-gravity machine." In general, though, readers are subconsciously turned off by seeing a negative and they relate this to your product. Find a way to turn statements in a positive direction. "Never Miss a Compliance Deadline - With KVP's Compli Software," becomes, "Beat Compliance Deadlines Cold with KVP's Compli Software."

- **Add specifics.** As you've seen in the case study chapters, the use of specifics is integral to capturing and holding a reader's attention. Without overloading, sprinkle them throughout your headlines and subheads to give the reader a clear thread to your article even if they don't read the full document at that moment.

Regarding the typography of your headlines
- Keep your headline/title to one line if possible. Use your subhead to fill-out the balance of the information.
- Capitalize all the important words and the last one (even if it isn't important.)

Write a Masterful Headline

- Use all-caps rarely. Legibility is reduced when everything is capitalized because the shape of the word becomes rectangular rather than its recognized word shape to the reader's eye.

NEVER MISS A COMPLIANCE DEADLINE

Never Miss a Compliance Deadline

Often if the body text uses a serif font such as Times New Roman, the titles are in a sans serif such as Arial – and vice versa.

- Reversed type (white on a colored background) is more difficult to read and ...

ALL CAPPED REVERSED TYPE IS OFTEN SKIPPED ENTIRELY BY THE READER

Use this format sparingly.

DO IT!
To get started, pick a section and give yourself five to ten minutes to write it. No more or you'll start second guessing and re-writing. We're after a draft here. You can't get it perfect the first time – so don't try.
- Keep going until you've finished writing the whole case study.
- We'll concentrate on polishing your prose in the next chapter.

8: Polish Your Prose

At last you can have some fun! In this chapter I've given you a plan of action for reviewing your work and a list of my top ten sentence strengthening tips to make your document ready for publication. Let's get started!

Surviving the Revision Cycle

Every draft needs two or more edits to make it sound professional. Start with the first one yourself then pass the work over to your in-house reviewers – and try to forget about it.

There is a catch to this, unfortunately. The more reviewers on your team – the more revision notes you'll have to endure. This usually has little bearing at all on the quality of your writing. It stems from the human condition where everyone thinks what they have to say is better than what someone else has written. To shield yourself, whether you work as an employee or as a freelancer for a company, be firm in your request to have one contact to work with who consolidates the feedback for you. If three or four people send you conflicting edits, all you'll have is a dog's breakfast in place of your story. Your structure will be gone and your logical flow of one sentence to the next will be gone too.

8: Polish Your Prose

No one understands this document the way you do. Remember this!

Specifically – and I can't stress this enough – the more edits you receive, the more chance errors in content, duplication of wording, critical omissions, grammar, context, and punctuation will be introduced too. Few non-editors, helpfully making suggestions on a co-worker's story, ever re-read the entire paragraph taking these factors into account. And even fewer understand the logic structure you've developed that holds the piece together in the first place. I've seen case studies and lengthy reports crash to bits because reviewers (often a boss, unfortunately) wanted to add-in their thoughts. The cohesiveness splintered.

This story is yours. Take creative criticism to make it better. Question anything you feel is incorrect. And remember the buck stops at you. Double-check that a sentence still makes sense – that the paragraph still means the same thing – and that the whole tone and logic of your story hasn't been changed. One wrong word can change everything. No exaggeration. Then formulate your plan to stand by it – do the changes that make the piece stronger, explain your thought processes to superiors before blindly accepting a bad change, and understand – unless you own the company – sometimes you'll have to clench your teeth and sacrifice a little.

Your first pass

Stepping away from the case study for a day or two after writing it would be ideal. In an office, we seldom have this luxury so at least try to go for a coffee, read something entirely different to break your mind set, and re-print the case study in an entirely different font. Perhaps set it up on a page with a photo. Do anything you can to make it look like a published piece you haven't seen before.

Surviving the Revision Cycle

This will force your eyes to read each word and push the memory back so you're interacting with the words as you read and not reciting what you've re-read forty times already.

When you're ready to get started, go back and review the document one more time for flow of logic. This time, don't read the individual words as much as soak up what each sentence and paragraph means. One idea should flow into the next making logical transitions from idea to idea and paragraph to paragraph. If they don't, move the sentences around until they make sense. If you've followed the case study template or your own pre-defined structure for other documents, this should be a quick process for a short document.

Strengthen your writing

I wanted to give you a tip sheet – something you can work through during your revision instead of trying to memorize a set of grammar rules. In fact, most of these tips don't deal with grammar as much as provide tricks to strengthen what you've written. Topics such as subject-verb agreement can easily fill a chapter in themselves. So think of each of the following list points in the way it was meant – as an introduction into the vast crafts of writing and editing. (And enjoy the bonus notes on the *Stories your teacher told you!*)

The Ten Tips to Strengthening Your Writing list (remember how a top 10 list makes people feel more at ease?) are the first points I look at in every document I review.

So, photocopy the condensed tips list (Page 88–89), pour a coffee, tea, or soda, and get ready to polish. The more you practice these tips on your work, the more ingrained they'll become and soon you'll be integrating them as you write. Watch as your thoughts on your writing go from, "Hmm, that came out not too badly," to "Hey, did I really write that?"

8: Polish Your Prose

Ten Tips to Strengthening Your Writing

I've included explanations and samples here and followed this section with a condensed list of the 10 items you can photocopy or find at **www.learnit-doit.com/cstemp10.html**.

1. **Active versus passive** – The active voice is more energetic and direct. The reader zooms along getting caught up in your story. Here, emphasis is placed on the person or thing doing the action. Rule of thumb: Always use the active voice unless you have a specific reason not to.

   Active: The vice president hired a new marketing manager.

   Active: The wind turbine generated sufficient energy to power half the city.

   In the passive voice, emphasis is placed on the receiver of the action. The pace of the document slows and can become wordy. Because the active doer isn't always revealed, a passive sentence can be confusing. But they have a few important uses, too. Choose the passive under these conditions:

   - When the doer of the action is difficult to determine or is unimportant.

     Passive: No solution was recommended.

   - When you want to emphasize the object or activity of the sentence.

     Passive: The computer was smashed by the falling bookshelf.

   - Conversely, use the passive when you want to de-emphasize the action doer.

     Passive: The citizens were irritated by the noisy wind turbines.

Ten Tips to Strengthening Your Writing

- When the passage you are writing has lots of action, a passive sentence helps slow it down so your readers can take a break or absorb what they've read.

2. **Verb choice** – If you've ever been coached in writing, no doubt you know the importance of using strong verbs. Though in school we were taught to use plenty of adjectives and adverbs in description – professional writers use them sparingly to keep their sentences lean and quick to read. We do this by choosing the right noun, and more so, the right verb to provide the intent of the sentence without too much explanation. In earlier chapters of this book we talked about using specifics – verb choice is just the same. Here are a few examples:

Weak: Marshall ran quickly down the hall and bumped into the professor blocking the doorway.

What kind of run was that? How hard did he bump? We know Marshall moved along fast – but we have no emotional attachment to this…and we know how important it is to bring the reader into your story through emotion, right? (See page 64, Use All the Senses)

Stronger: Marshall charged down the hall and bashed into the professor blocking the doorway.

Marshall really, really wanted to get where he was going and no one was stopping him!

Or: Marshall sprinted down the hallway scraping past the professor blocking the doorway.

Marshall is an athlete – probably agile and most likely not fat if he could get through the blocked door. Notice how charged and sprinted give you a different visual?

8: Polish Your Prose

One of the worst transgressors of verb choice is the verb *to be*. When we write quickly – or when we're not motivated by the topic – *to be* verbs pop up all over the place. Go back and look at what you've written and see if a stronger verb would better serve the sentence. We don't want every instance changed or your work will look like it fell out of a thesaurus, but a few more powerful verbs will give your work life.

This **is** a situation where we'll need to call-in the vice president.
This situation requires contacting the vice president.

There **was** a good connection between the manager and his trainee.
The manager and his trainee connected perfectly.

3. **Subject-verb agreement** – One of the most maligned but trickiest topics to grasp is subject-verb agreement. Grammar and style books devote pages to the rules and exceptions and I'll leave them to it if you'd like a full explanation. For our purposes – I'll point out a few spots that could trip you up.

We'll tackle this backwards and look only at the exceptions. We already know if a subject is singular – the verb will reflect this. If a subject is plural, the verb will be also.

The book is on the desk.
The books are on the desk.

Problems arise when we don't know if the subject is singular or plural or when exceptions arise. Here are a few:

Ten Tips to Strengthening Your Writing

- Pronouns that always take the singular:
  Each – every – anyone – no one – either – everyone
  Everyone here **is** going to the meeting.

- Compound subjects joined by *and* take the plural:
  Griffin and Oscar **are** going to the trade show.

- Compound subjects joined by *or* must always agree with the subject closest to the verb:

  The desk or the chairs **are** ready for painting.
  The chairs or the desk **is** ready for painting.

- Collective nouns take the singular if the group functions as a unit and take the plural when referring to the parts of the group.

  The jury **was** dismissed for lunch. The staff **was** told the new president's name.

  The jury **were** arguing over the verdict. The staff **were** working-out their schedules.

4. ***It is* and *there are*** –Also known as "expletives" (truly!), these words temporarily take the place of the subject. As often as possible, give your sentences more strength by re-writing them without these introductory words:

   Weak: There is no money in this year's budget to hire an editor.

   Stronger: We have no money in this year's budget to hire an editor. (Make it active! Provide someone who does the action.)

   Or: No money is available in this year's budget to hire an editor.

8: Polish Your Prose

Weak: It's often difficult to find alternate wording for a sentence.

Stronger: Finding alternate wording for a sentence is often difficult.

Or: I find rewording a sentence is often difficult. (Make it active!)

5. **That** – Time and again I've read about authors who submitted their book to a publisher and were told to cut it by up to several thousand words. One of the first steps they take is to make a global search of the word *that* and delete as many as possible without affecting clarity or grammar. Most people don't realize how many times *that* appears in their writing until they're told to go look.

    Watch how removing *that* and tightening the sentences further strengthens them:

    If the puppy is very tiny, ensure that the box is safe and that it won't tip over on him. Take the lid off and set the box on its side with a towel inside. Help him to understand that's where he can sleep during the day.

    If the puppy is tiny, ensure the box is safe and won't tip over on him. Take the lid off and set the box on its side with a towel inside. Help the pup understand this is his daytime sleeping spot.

6. **Problems with modifiers** – Whether misplaced or dangling the result is the same. If you don't place the modifier as close as possible to what it modifies, confusion occurs. Have a look:

    Incorrect: Typing furiously, my dog left the room.

    Correct: While I typed furiously, my dog left the room.

    Or: My dog left the room while I typed furiously.

Ten Tips to Strengthening Your Writing

You'll find this problem especially when using introductory phrases, as we just saw in an obvious example, but it happens in business writing all the time and we often wonder why something just doesn't sound right.

Incorrect: Keeping our customers in mind, our services focus on quality materials, and on-time delivery.

When was the last time a service could keep anything in mind?

Correct: Keeping our customers in mind, we focus on service, quality materials, and on-time delivery.

Or to play it safe and speed it up, drop the introductory phrase:

We keep our customers in mind with quality service, materials, and on-time delivery.

7. **Unclear antecedents*** – Along the same lines, we need to keep pronouns as close as possible to the noun they replace. When in doubt, recast the sentences. (*An antecedent is the word the pronoun replaces.)

   Incorrect: George gave the presentation to his boss. He'd felt nervous for hours beforehand.

   Why was George's boss nervous? Although it's likely the writer meant George felt nervous, the word *he'd* in the next sentence is looking for someone to cling to... and found the boss first! This problem often results in miscommunication.

   Correct: George felt nervous for hours before giving his presentation to the boss.

8: Polish Your Prose

8. **Faulty parallelism** – One of the quickest ways to polish your work is to keep a series of words parallel in structure. This means the series or list must all start the same, such as with nouns, verbs, adjectives, or adverbs. Don't worry, you can do this by ear most of the time:

   Incorrect: Before the conference, make sure the water cooler is full, that you make coffee, and all the pencils are sharpened.

   Correct: Before the conference, ensure the water cooler is full, the coffee is made, and all the pencils are sharpened.

9. **Repetition, redundancy, and padding.** I know, I'm bundling a few issues into one tip but they all result in taking up valuable space without offering further information to your story. Spotting and correcting these problems goes a long way to polishing your text.

   Repetition is the easiest of the three to wipe out. If you have a solid structure, you'll never have to worry about repetition. You'll know exactly what points go into each paragraph and what purpose they serve to your message. Repetition can sneak up on you through revisions, however. When someone helpfully changes (or replaces!) one of your sentences, check to see if you've already expressed that idea in a different way in another place.

   Redundancy is similar to repetition but is generally used in two or three words.

   You'll see many redundancies in ad copy – where marketing-speak stretches the rules of English often to good effect. But for everyday text, don't use them! Here is a short list. You'll find dozens more if you look:

Ten Tips to Strengthening Your Writing

- Free gift – A gift is always free.
- PDF format – The full term is Portable Document Format so adding *format* afterward is unnecessary.
- Such as…etc. – Example: Add vegetables such as carrots, beans, corn, etc. (Choose one or the other.)
- The reason is because – Instead, use, "the reason is that."
- Big in size
- Return back
- Close proximity
- Follow after
- Young baby

Padding comes in two forms. One is when the writer fills up the page with too many modifiers or too much description. The other form is called circumlocution. This happens when three, four, or more words can be replaced by one. Here is a short sample:

- In order to = to (What does "in order" mean? Does anyone know?)
- At this point in time = now
- In spite of the fact = although
- Take into consideration = consider

10. **What's In It For Me? (WIIFM)**
    I've saved the best for last – because often the last thing in a list is the longest remembered. And if this is the only point you recall from the whole book, it's also one of the most important.

    In the general mechanics of writing, this won't help your grammar. But to make any piece of writing stronger, if

8: Polish Your Prose

you always think of your reader, and write to them, you'll stay on message and not be tempted by the tangent you'd love to pursue. This in turn tightens your writing.

- Look for what the customer, prospect, or general reader wants from your product, service, or information. It's often not the feature or benefit you want to tell them about. Know your audience.
- Give them free information in blogs and articles.
- Make your company the go-to source of information for this item or service.

In short – make life easier for your customer and they'll reward you for it.

Now for a little fun...

Stories your teacher told you! Or, *yes,* you may use split infinitives, begin a sentence with *and* or *but,* and end a sentence with a preposition.

Amazing but true, *splitting infinitives* does not break a grammatical rule. These gems happen when you separate *to* from the verb. Split infinitives are often used for emphasis, such as the famous Star Trek phrase: "To boldly go." In Latin, infinitives are one word and this is where the concept came from. English isn't Latin, though, and we have two-word infinitives that can be split.

And yes, you may begin a sentence with *and, but, also, or,* and *however.* Beginning a sentence with *but* can even show strength of conviction.

Ten Tips to Strengthening Your Writing

What about the rule that says *ending a sentence with a preposition* is wrong? According to *Merriam-Webster's Concise Dictionary of English Usage* – and grammarian authorities – this rule is also entirely false. It appears we owe this incorrect pearl of wisdom to the 17th-century poet John Dryden, who most likely reflected upon Latin usage as well. In fact, not using a preposition at the end of a sentence can often make it sound pompous.

There you have it. For a tip sheet you can use on-the-fly, I've listed the ten tips on the next page.

8: Polish Your Prose

Ten Tips to Strengthening Your Writing

1. Active versus passive (Active is more energetic.) Use it!
   Active: The vice president hired a new marketing manager.
   Passive: The computer was smashed by the falling bookshelf.

2. Verb choice (Choose for strength of meaning.)
   Weak: Marshall ran quickly down the hall and bumped...
   Stronger: Marshall charged down the hall and bashed...

3. Subject-verb agreement
   Singular: The book is on the desk.
   Plural: The books are on the desk.

4. *It is* and *there are* (Revise when possible.)
   Weak: There is no money in this year's budget to hire an editor.
   Stronger: We have no money in this year's budget to hire an editor.

5. That (Overuse)
   If the puppy is tiny, ensure *that* the box is safe and *that* it won't tip over on him. (Delete both.)

6. Problems with modifiers (Keep them near what they modify.)
   Incorrect: Typing furiously, my dog left the room.
   Correct: While I typed furiously, my dog left the room.

7. Unclear antecedents (Keep them near what they modify.)
   Incorrect: George gave his presentation to his *boss*. *He'd* felt nervous for hours beforehand.
   Correct: George felt nervous for hours before giving his presentation to the boss.

8. Faulty parallelism (Keep a series parallel)
   Faulty: ...make sure the water cooler is full, that you make coffee, and all the pencils are sharpened.
   Correct: ...ensure the water cooler is full, the coffee is made, and all the pencils are sharpened.

Ten Tips to Strengthening Your Writing

9. Repetition, redundancy, and padding
   (Tighten your writing by eliminating words that don't directly add to your message.)

10. What's in it for me? / WIIFM (Make life easier for your customer by giving them the information they want.)

Look for a downloadable copy of this list at **www.learnit-doit.com/cstemp10.html** .

DO IT!

Once you've written your case study, make a copy of the *Ten Tips to Strengthening Your Writing* and check off each point as you polish your text.

After sending your document for editing, ensure the integrity of logic isn't ruined through other people's changes. This is critical. A single word has the power to change everything.

- Do you need a transition sentence anywhere?
- Are the sentences clear in meaning?
- Could you tighten them using the techniques in this chapter?

In the next part of the book we'll look at using the same information you gathered for your case study and adapting it to five other marketing documents. When the time comes for writing and editing each – be ready with your ten tips!

Part Two

Add Media Releases, Articles, Blogs, eblasts, and Handouts to Your Case Studies for a Complete Marketing Campaign

Successful marketing campaigns ensure your message is widely distributed in as many ways as possible to reach potential customers.

Case studies are one vehicle; articles, blog posts, and hand-outs are others; and eblasts and media releases are your worker-bees in distributing those messages to your target audience.

This section of the book looks at using the material you've already researched and helps you put it towards these five additional documents in your marketing kit.

The following sections take you through a basic structure for each document type. We'll look at ways your case study material could fit and where you can add, refine, or retarget the information, and why.

Think about these documents before setting out on your case study interview. Pre-planning will help you compile questions additional to what you'll need immediately and avoid calling your client a second time.

Enjoy!

9: Trade Show & Sales Handouts

Make your case study do double duty. When you use it as a handout, you bring your story to your audience in an enticing new venue. People at trade shows or potential customers your sales team visit are already in your target audience group.

A handout presented to an interested visitor at your booth immediately creates interest and serves as a conversation starter. Take advantage of every moment you have your visitors' attention and turn three seconds into fifteen during the hand-off. Explain, briefly, what's on each side *before* handing it across to them. You want them to see your headline, which should pop off the page with information, before the sheet is shoved into the black hole of the handouts bag.

> The best part of a case study handout is you don't have to write a thing. This is the only time you'll read this for the rest of the book – so take advantage of it!

Of course, you *can* revise the study if you wish – but especially if it was kept to a single page, all you need do is add a little color and a few photos and you're done. Longer studies might need both sides of the page or editing to reduce it to one page. In either case, make sure you've got plenty of white space to invite

9: Trade Show & Sales Handouts

the reader in. The handout is a true marketing piece so enjoy the extra pizzazz.

Use the reverse side of a single-page case study handout to provide more details on the product or service used in the study. Again – add photos. Refer to the study to make the connection with the product or service, such as in a features and benefits list. The visitor will see exactly what options drew the case study customer to act. A quote also catches a visitor's eye. This brings-in much needed third-party credibility. Use quotes wherever you have a space or want to open-up a heavy block of text.

Potential customers are always on the lookout for what makes life easier for them, the "What's in it for me? (WIIFM)" appeal of your product. Your case study showed *one* focus solving *one* crucial problem for *one* customer. Be certain to address a variety of problem-solution scenarios on side two. You might just hit on the very one your booth visitor experiences.

A note on photos

Poor quality photos do more of a disservice to your company than not including them at all. If you print your own handouts (or have someone take them to the copy shop for you) – ensure the photos are clear and sharp by printing directly from the computer file. *Never allow anyone to photocopy a handout with photos in them.* Make it an immutable law of your company!

> **DO IT!**
> Look through your case studies and choose one or two that tell a visual story. The more eye-catching the photos – the longer you have your reader's attention.
>
> Send them for design in-house or at a design studio, and you'll be ready for any final input during the crunch days prior to a trade show.

10: Media Releases

The media release (also known as a press release) is a brilliant way to put your product or service in front of hundreds – or hundreds of thousands – of readers. To get there, you've got two hurdles to cross:
- Attracting and holding the editor's attention long enough to say yes to publishing your message
- Once published, attracting and holding the reader's attention long enough for them to contact you

Attracting the Editor's Attention

Your story will beat hundreds of releases crossing an editor's desk just by keeping it simple, clean, and well written.
- Use white paper or a white background on your electronic file. (See the section on formatting.)
- Use the headline and subhead to say what the press release is about.
- Find a news hook or interesting angle. Newspapers have no interest in advertising your product or service for free. If the release isn't newsworthy to the publication, it has no value to them.
- Keep it factual and free of hype.

10: Media Releases

Attracting and Holding the Reader's Attention

If the editor uses the hook you wrote for the headline and subheads, or writes something better, you've already got a great start in attracting readers to your company.

Next, it's your job to hold them with the structure and content of your release and you'll do this by pulling material from your case study and interview material. You've already collected the best of the best information – let's take it to the media.

Why Write a Media Release?

Visibility, **credibility**, and **sales** of your product or service are the top three reasons for writing a media release. To achieve all three within one page of writing takes an understanding of the goal of the release and planning-out the content to achieve it.

Visibility – Not long ago our only avenue for distributing a media release was newspapers or magazines and a select number of businesses. You were shackled by the mail – which over the years gave way to faxing – and eventually to e-mail. Sourcing publications and the editors' names was a huge task and one you had to work diligently at to keep current or your media release could be tossed out by a new editor (in a high turnover industry) for being addressed to her predecessor.

Not all of this has changed. Personalization is still absolutely the best way to network, but names and e-mails at papers and companies have become a highly guarded secret in today's spam-filled cyber waves. In general publications, we often have

Why Write a Media Release?

to settle for the editor@ address and play the odds. The volume of publications is your friend in these cases.

Contact information for thousands of papers and magazines are within your reach on the Internet. Online (broadcast) releases are also an option for free or a fee and are often industry-specific.

You can make your product visible to hundreds of thousands of people...*if* the media release is picked up for publication. This doesn't mean you should stop writing for your audience. These people are your most likely buyers and if the writing of your release reflects their interest, they'll read-on. For general readership magazines, stay away from jargon and keep your writing clear so everyone understands your message and newcomers aren't intimidated.

To break into new sectors, analyze the audience you're targeting and revise your marketing materials accordingly. Media releases for water pumps going to swimming pool builders as well as industrial waste companies would require different hooks and anecdotes.

Now that you've caught the attention of your audience, keep it by gaining their trust.

Credibility – A media release, one picked up by a publication and not self-posted to a free media release directory, offers built-in credibility. We presume a journalist has taken the time to research beyond the backgrounder and the managing editor has approved the story.

Third party quotes also increase credibility and raise the trust factor of your product.

10: Media Releases

Once you've given readers a reason to believe, you move into the sale.

Sales – Be careful here. Sales copy is NOT what newspapers want to see. They're interested in news stories and only a story with a news angle – relevant to their readers will do. If an editor sees a hint of marketing in your media release, she won't use it, and this could hurt future legitimate releases by your company. However, attracting attention to your product or service is exactly why you've sent the release to them, so how do you make this a win-win for the editor and your company?

Write a product information release if it makes sense for your product. Do your research to see who prints a product information column in their magazine and buy a copy. Do your best to find a contact name, as the field will be small and you'll want to build that base of editors. You *must* keep your contact list for this group updated and be ready to adjust your releases to fit their schedules and space.

Check the publication's online writing guidelines or contact the magazine (not the editor you'll be pitching to!) to see what topics they want and the format they prefer.

The approach most often used to catch the editor's eye is

Exception: Product Releases

Certain commercial and consumer magazines cater specifically to people looking to buy. Camera and computer magazines are an example. Product editors reserve space to include the scoop on the latest lenses and laptops.

For these magazines, write a short description of the product and include a few bullet points of features or technology readers will want to know.

Take time to learn the style of these magazines and follow their format for submissions.

If you make it easy to cut and paste and add pre-sized photos – your releases could leap-frog ahead of your competitors'.

What is the Goal of Your Media Release?

to hook your product to a current news item or trend. We'll talk about how to do this later in the chapter.

When a sale isn't a sale

Sales aren't always quantified by money. The appeal you want in your marketing media releases could occasionally be a call for action of a different sort.

If you send out a release to raise awareness of an environmental issue, for example, and you want people to come together as a group, then your *sale* is the number of participants showing up for your rally.

Introducing a new employee to the industry through a media release says, "Meet our newest team member. Come see how working with him makes buying easy."

As in any marketing document, the media release must still focus on what it can do to make life easier for the reader. Even if all that is, is to give away free information – and imprint your name on the customer once again.

What is the Goal of Your Media Release?

You already know you want to raise visibility, add credibility, and increase sales. Now you decide exactly what the purpose of this release is and where you can use the information you have already compiled from your case study.

Let's say your company has just released new insurance software that enables companies to offer a portal for brokers to get instant quotes for the consumer. You've written a case study on the experiences of one test company and one particular concern they faced. Now you're ready to go public with the product.

10: Media Releases

Where is your focus and who are you speaking to? In this instance you have several options:

Focus on:	Audience:
The portal software	To catch the attention of insurance companies, you could concentrate on product ability through features and benefits and just mention the success story from the case study. This works well particularly if you're focusing on the full portal software for the media release but the case study narrows the focus to only one function of the software.
The case study story	To catch the attention of insurance companies AND individual brokers/agents, concentrate on credibility through a third party. Here is where your case study shines. The brokers see the huge benefits in costs and time savings by dealing with insurance companies who offer your portal service. A few of the product details will be forfeited to the fact sheet in this version and quotes are a must.
Your company	Perhaps you're trying to raise your company's brand recognition and the portal software is your big ticket item. Tie the product to a news hook to catch the attention of the media, but lean heavily on your company's service and reputation. For example, a particularly bad season for storms would be a good time to send out a media release that offers consumers ways to protect themselves. Mention how several insurance companies offer instant coverage through a new portal system hooked directly with their neighborhood insurance agent.

By understanding the goal of who you want to focus on and what they want to know, you can slant the content of your media release, or any document, in that direction.

How to Format Your Media Release

Not long ago, the media would not accept media releases sent by fax or e-mail. Now e-mail is the widely accepted route and this presents a change in the way the releases are presented. I've outlined both formats for you here.

Paper – Use only white paper, never colored or printed with a design. In the past, editors preferred blank instead of letterhead to conserve space and we put the relevant information up top where it could be easily found.

This requirement for simplicity – including a white background – is just as important in an e-mail.

Font – The rule of thumb is to use a sans-serif font for the screen (Arial, Verdana) and a serif font for paper (Times New Roman, Courier.) The little "feet" on the serif font letters help the eye move from letter to letter and join into a recognizable shape, which is the word. Curiously, when we look at a lit monitor our eyes need more clarity and the san-serif fonts without the feet work better for legibility. Having said that – many sans-serif fonts that aren't too wide, such as Calibri and Verdana are often used in printed newsletters and other shorter documents with great success and eye appeal.

Keep the font size average and the line space (the space between the rows of words) wider than the automatic space your software installs. Larger font sizes actually lead to reduced legibility.

Line and paragraph spacing – On paper, double-space your lines and tab twice to indent for each paragraph. By e-mail, use regular line spacing.

Heading – This is the area above the actual media release and should include the following information for the editor to see immediately:

10: Media Releases

Media Release

FOR IMMEDIATE RELEASE

Photos: 2 x 300 dpi jpegs attached:
mycar.jpg, mydog.jpg

Contact:
Paula Wheeler, Writer
B: (555)-555-5555
C: (555)-555-5555
my-mail@my-mail.com

Breakdown of the header area

Media Release – I put this in large letters at the top of the page and in the subject line of the e-mail (or on the envelope) along with the short headline to alert the editor of time-sensitive newsworthy information.

Follow this with FOR IMMEDIATE RELEASE – or FOR RELEASE ON [DATE], to alert the editor of the release's timing. This is placed on the left side of the page. It's better, of course, not to rely on sending the releases out too early. Since you'll most likely send it by e-mail now anyway, simply have everything ready to go in advance and distribute the release on the correct date for *immediate release*. By controlling the time of release yourself, the information won't slip out to the public too early in error or be missed entirely because the editor couldn't get to her follow-up file for a few days.

> **NOTE:** Never write, *For Immediate Publication*. This implies you are telling the paper or magazine what to publish. Always keep in mind you are hoping they will pick it up, but it's their publication, and their decision.

How to Format Your Media Release

Placing **contact information** in the top right corner is vital. Often journalists and editors need to verify a fact before going to print and if they can't reach a contact day or evening, they will likely drop the release. Formerly, we put a day and evening phone number down for the main contact. Now we often include a business and cell number. Deadlines can run late into the evening. Ensure you've made it simple for an editor to find you during those days around the release launch.

If you've included a photo, mention this in the space below For Immediate Release.

The news hook or interesting angle
Without a hook, the editor has no reason to consider your release nor the reader to read it. For the wind turbines discussed in chapter three, the writer mentions a debate on the noise of turbines, a topic surfacing in towns and local news as more turbine sites are chosen. The turbines from our writer's company are quieter, so tapping-into this issue might give them not only a story of their own but mention in a sidebar or feature article written by national papers.

More often, the world's news doesn't comply with your company timetable and you have to be creative. If your announcement is news in your eyes – make it news for other people too! Do a little research. Look into historical events for your region, country or overseas and tap into an anniversary. Broaden the scope – in the case of the wind turbine, perhaps an alternate energy conference is coming. If quietness is the biggest feature – add information on noise and health. Find what stirs people's emotions and work with it. Keep it factual, don't use sales language, and people will be interested.

Read about Google Alerts on page 145 for additional ways to find news hooks.

10: Media Releases

The headline and subhead

I've discussed headlines in the writing section of this book, though I'd like to touch on the focus of a headline in a media release. You want to raise interest – but in this case you must do it with factual information and not a teaser. Editors quite often change headlines to suit the article they'll write from your media release. Even if they do, you still need to sell the story to them in the first place so put sufficient thought into your headings.

Your main headline needs to state the facts in as few words as possible. The fewer the words the larger the type size you can use. And headlines should never wrap a line if possible!

The subhead flows from the headline, adding more information and drawing the reader into the body copy. Try keeping this to two lines maximum. Remember that all capitals are less legible than lower-case type.

The reverse pyramid

Think of a pyramid-shaped container that lets you remove the top like a lid and fill it with your favorite soup. What happens? All the lovely chicken and vegetables fall to the bottom and the container fills with the broth right to the top.

In a media release, we want that quality meat and potatoes substance at the top. You've got three to five seconds to grab the editor's attention and not much longer to pull him into your release. You start with an informational headline and subhead and move quickly into what the release is about. This is the base of your pyramid – the most important ingredients in your soup. You've flipped the pyramid upside down and now you've got a lot of information to relate in a short paragraph or two. Here's how you do it.

How to Format Your Media Release

Start with every journalist's standby – the 6 W's. Who, what, where, when, why... and how (Close enough - *how* technically still has a w in it!) If you've written a newsy heading and subhead, you've most likely included a few of the w's already. In the first paragraph, or two at the most, use the balance of w's as applicable to your topic.

For example:

Plucki Chicken Fritters Opens Three Locations in Chicago
Tremendous growth encourages fast food restaurant
to expand operations

- Who = Plucki Chicken Fritters
- What = Opens Three Locations
- Where = Chicago
- When = Weekend of the 15-17 (first paragraph)
- Why = Tremendous growth encourages expansion
- How = With a grand opening (first paragraph)

Here's a suggestion for the first paragraph, leading from the headings:

April 11, 20XX – Chicago, Illinois – Plucki Chicken Fritters is pleased to announce their grand opening special this weekend, April 15 - 17, by giving away a single order of free fritters for every family pack ordered.

As the release continues down the page, the information becomes less crucial to the topic. If the editor stops at paragraph three, he's not losing anything of importance. Media releases are not the place for the surprise conclusion or a quote at the end geared to elicit a strong reaction. If it's important – it needs to go to the top of the page.

10: Media Releases

This reverse pyramid format was developed back when layouts were mocked-up in paper and your release would be cut and pasted in the real sense. This was why letterhead was a nuisance because the top had to be cut off – and why the contact info was needed up top because if room was tight, the bottom of the page was also cut off. The format still makes sense for busy editors, so we raise our chances of being picked from the hundreds of media releases crossing their desks by making life easy for them and following their format. (Remember WIIFM? This applies to editors too. Make it easy.)

Quotes and your media release

Keep in mind, the nature of the media release is that it provides newsworthy material for a publication's readers. If it looks like a marketing piece, it won't be picked up. This can appear to make your job as a writer difficult when broadcasting the wonderful attributes of your new product. But you've got a trick up your sleeve – the wonderful quotes by your case study customers. You can still use a quote from one of your own company executives, but you have to keep those focused on facts or they'll smack of narcissism.

Credibility – In the same way your case study gained credibility for you by having a customer speak about your product or service – the media release can raise your credibility too. If your customer is willing to include his contact details for information verification – your chances of publication grow even higher.

White space – Nothing is more intimidating to a reader than solid blocks of text in front of them. Authors of fiction know this and aim for plenty of dialogue dispersed among the narrative in their books. When dialogue isn't possible, they go for a series of shorter paragraphs to allow-in some light. You can do the same in your media release by including a quote or two.

How to Format Your Media Release

Personality – Quotes add a personal touch. We all prefer to hear information from someone else to get their opinion at a one-to-one level. A trust is built in reading a quote over reading a block of plain text telling us what we should believe.

First name or last…Who does the talking?
One of the simplest ways to achieve a tone in your writing is in how you address your characters. After always using the full name, and title if appropriate, the first time it appears in your story, what happens next?

Most newspapers and magazines use the last name only from then on. *You* aren't bound to this, though. Many smaller publications, striking a more casual or intimate tone with their readers, choose first names. Unless my client requests otherwise, I use first names in all my documents. I work hard to catch the readers' eye and draw them in, why would I suddenly take a step in the opposite direction?

Once again, look at your target audience. Think of your subject. Think of your message. Think of the goal of your piece. If it's a marketing document, first names usually work. If it's not, make a decision and boldy go!

Ending the media release
The press release itself doesn't have the space or need for a proper conclusion, but you do need to end with one more piece of information – your company blurb. This is generally a little pre-written paragraph your company uses in many communications and includes what the company does, potentially how big it is, when it was founded and if it is an award winner in any area.

If your release happens to be about a merger or acquisition, your company's blurb comes directly below the media release text followed by the acquired company's description.

10: Media Releases

The Media Release Backgrounder and Fact Sheet

Just because media releases are short doesn't mean you have to give up all the lovely details you've unearthed. In fact, if you've caught the editor's interest, you could find your media release handed to a journalist for a full article. Be prepared. For a little extra investment in time during the writing process, you can send additional information that backs-up your claims in the release or gives broader information on the news hook you've chosen. Remember, you've got a case study in hand so some of your work is done.

Backgrounder: This includes more information on your company, the product, the people, the case study – whatever relates to the topic of your media release. In the case of the insurance portal software, we'd include more details on the software, who in the industry uses it (with permission to mention their company!), and perhaps a few words on your company's history in this area. Keep it in point form on one page.

Fact sheet: This includes interesting facts outside your company. If you used a news hook on the growing trend of companies providing portals to their customers, give back-up here. Add statistics on portals. Quote percentages of how many consumers will purchase insurance on the spot in an office versus those sent home to wait for a quote. The idea is to show the journalist a story exists in all this and hope she mentions your company favorably. Keep the fact seet to one page but include links for follow-up to your sources.

11: e-mails and eblasts

Why Use Them?

Think of an e-mail as a letter or memo of correspondence between two or more individuals who know each other.

An eblast, much as its name implies, is a piece of e-correspondence blasted out to a mailing list of people. An eblast generally has more design and might look like a blog or newsletter. It could include two or three articles, possibly links to other articles, testimonials from clients, and a soft sales pitch to get you to visit their website. Large companies use eblasts to catch your attention with contests or coupons as well.

Both the e-mail and eblast have a purpose in distributing your message to an audience. Each is slightly different.

Solicited and Unsolicited e-mails and eblasts

Around about now, if you've never run a mail-out campaign and are new to the eblast idea, your mind has just exploded in thoughts of how many people you could reach this way. And imagine the cost savings? The rest of you are thinking...spam. You're both right.

11: e-mails and eblasts

In many regions, you can send a personalized message to someone you don't know offering your company's services and this is not considered spam. Personalization is key. The letter must contain more details about the company or person than can be found in a contact database.

If a letter is developed as a template with only minimal changes for dozens or thousands of recipients, it is no longer considered personal and you head into the dark waters of spam – **if** you are sending the letter to an **unsolicited** list of people.

For instance, if you've purchased a list from a chamber of commerce and the next day you send off an eblast to everyone with a couple of good articles and a promo for saving twenty percent on a customer's first purchase, this would be spam.

The good news is, you can send as many e-mails and eblasts with promos and product information as you wish to people on a **solicited** list. This is a list of people who have said "yes" to receiving e-mails from you. So how do you get one of these?

Building a List

To have a list...you must build a list. We'll talk about electronic opt-in forms in a moment, but depending on your business, to create a solicited e-mail list you look for ways to gather e-mail addresses with permission from the people owning them.

Performers, speakers, and other people in the public often have an e-mail sign-up book. They simply ask people to leave their name and e-mail address so the performer can contact the person about upcoming engagements. At trade shows you might leave your business card with the rep, which they later hand over to their marketing department. Restaurants and stores have business card draws for free meals and merchandise. Contest forms usually include a space for an e-mail address as a way of

Use Opt-in Forms to Create a List

getting in touch with the winner. In some regions you might need to specifically ask if the e-mail address may be used for sending future correspondence.

A little trick to help people feel more secure about giving their information is to ask for their first name only as well as the e-mail address. If your company sells online, too, the customer will expect to give full contact details at the point of sale anyway and those names will be sorted as part of your preferred list.

Use Opt-in Forms to Create a List

You've seen them and probably used these little opt-in forms a dozen times as you've surfed the Internet. Every time a website asks for your name and e-mail address, your information is being collected and put in a database for the future.

The opt-in form is a little piece of code placed right in a website or blog that stores names and e-mail addresses to a database. Third-party companies who provide these opt-in forms can manage lists of thousands of names, provide you with statistics, and generally take over the added work from your marketing department.

Through this service, you can continue to develop your list and service those on it through broadcast eblasts, targeted e-mails, or requested information from your website. These service companies provide opt-in forms and professional-looking eblast templates and they schedule your mail-outs, generate automatic responses to opt-ins, and provide you with statistics.

One of the most popular companies is AWeber Communications. You can reach them through this link:

http://www.kvp.aweber.com.

11: e-mails and eblasts

NOTE: Tell the person on your site what they're signing up for. As an example, say, "To receive our monthly newsletter, sign-up here," so they aren't concerned about what your purpose is. You might wish to say your company never rents or sells its lists to anyone – but be certain this is true before making the claim.

Unsubscribing - Even people who agree to receive your e-mails and eblasts may one day decide your information isn't quite what they're after anymore and they want to unsubscribe from further mailings. You must provide a way for them to do this, whether it's a matter of them e-mailing you back or clicking a link at the bottom of the eblast.

Use e-mails and eblasts to Your Advantage

Similar to regular posted mail, e-mails and eblasts tend to have greater results than websites in putting your company's information into the hands of potential clients. Mail and e-mail are similar because they both arrive in our mailbox. Websites on the other hand rely on someone to find your site and go to it.

Now that you have the e-mail address, and the eblast has been sent, the next task is to make sure it's opened!

Take advantage of your readers' initial attention to draw them into the body of the e-mail or eblast. Use the tools we discussed in the case study chapters:

- Create a headline that hooks and a subhead that guides the reader into the body text.
- Offer something free to make life easier. (WIIFM)
- Tread lightly if at all with sales pitches in e-mails and eblasts. Instead, give away information and provide links to your website. Readers quickly unsubscribe to e-mails filled with marketing pitches.

Target Companies with Personalized Correspondence

- Send eblasts frequently enough to keep your company in your audience's mind but not so often as to irritate them. Marketers say every three to four weeks is good. With all the e-mail I receive, I'd prefer five or six weeks.
- Keep your introduction and articles short and get to the point immediately. An e-mail should run 150 words at most and your eblast – if it has a number of articles – should provide a newsy opening paragraph for each and link to the balance of the article on your website.

Target Companies with Personalized Correspondence

eblasts are wonderful if you have a list, but what if you want to target a number of companies and don't have a list? We do this with personalized correspondence. This does NOT include dropping a name and title into a template and sending it to 50 companies ten minutes later. That's still spam. Instead, mention details of their business, a current event that ties to your message and relates to their industry, or follow-up on a media release you've read from them. Let them see you've made an effort to get to know them. Make it personal. It takes more time, but the work is worth the effort.

Know who you are writing to

Do your research. Find the name and title of the person you wish to reach. Networking through associations and word of mouth is one of the best ways to find accurate information. Social media sites also help provide you with names and often have more recent and accurate information. Browsing the Internet helps but isn't always accurate, though the temptation is great. Cold calling is, unfortunately, another way.

What you might have a problem securing is the e-mail address. Most receptionists will give you a name and title but they draw the line at the e-mail – for good reason. Consider starting with a mailed letter to the contact person in these cases, and ask for an e-mail during your follow-up call. (You don't need to ask for it outright. Offer to send information the person might find interesting based on your conversation...your case study for example. Remember the WIIFM rule!)

Using Your Case Study in an e-mail or eblast

Use your case study as a jumping-off point to generate and send a personalized e-mail or eblast to your contact list.

In a personalized e-mail, your purpose is to entice readers to contact you and get a conversation going. Mention a point of interest from the study and invite the person to either click a link to be sent a copy of the full case study or to e-mail you personally with the request.

For a general eblast, include the first paragraph from the case study or write a paragraph that paraphrases a few points and hooks readers. You could include a link from this to the page on your website where the case study sits. At the end of the case study page, provide links directly to the products on your site you discussed.

Another way is to ask the reader to sign-in and have the case study sent to them. This makes use of the opt-in form for future statistics.

The important point is to hook the reader's attention and especially in posted mail to obtain the e-mail address for your list. The best way? Give the readers something free, and make their life easier.

This discussion is meant as a guide only. Please check with your individual country and region for spam laws, which differ everywhere and are being constantly changed as spammers learn new ways to get around the laws.

12: Articles

For Newsletters, Magazines, and Advertorials

Articles are an important part of your marketing campaign. You can write them to tell the same story as your case study, offer an alternate perspective on the project, or use a portion of the material you gathered for an entirely different article and audience. Articles use additional distribution methods as your case studies for a broader reach and they complement your case studies within the full marketing campaign portfolio.

The art of article writing can fill a book, so for our purposes here I've chosen the most likely form you'd choose for a marketing package – a basic short article using a story structure. This can be adapted for use in consumer and trade magazines, e-zines, newsletters, and advertorials.

Why Write an Article?

Articles bring information about your company to a new audience and in a different format from case studies and media releases. Bylines or company names embedded in an article help raise the credibility and visibility of your firm and your products. Unlike an advertorial where you've paid to publish your article and can use marketing language and promote your products freely, an

12: Articles

article is generally expected to show both sides of a story or at least not be biased toward a particular product, so the article represents a non-sales venue for you, but an important one nonetheless.

Remind Your Readers About Who You Are

The rule of thumb for creating a long-term memory is to experience something in as many ways and as many times as possible.

By reaching-out through the Web, in advertising, in articles, and on television and radio, if that's a viable choice, your chances of being recognized increases substantially.

Articles, along with your case study, handouts, media releases, blog, and eBlasts serve the purpose of spreading this network of experiences for readers to see and absorb. And except for the advertorial – the cost is negligible.

Writing to Your Audience

Your audience extends from your current customers and the industry sector your company works within, to the general public who read your article in a magazine or ezine, and especially to audience groups where you'd like to expand.

All these readers find certain topics more interesting than others and will be more or less familiar with each. Expect to write to different levels of expertise pending the publication you target.

Just as you did with the media release, determine the purpose you want to achieve with your article and who you want to direct it to prior to blocking-out the structure.

Structuring the Article

You'll notice similarities and differences in the structure you've learned for a case study to that of an article. Case study readers expect the material laid-out in a particular format. Even so, the structure doesn't dictate the content and you've learned you can infuse it with the story structure we've come to know in books, television shows, and movies to bring it to life.

Short articles also have a structure and they too follow the hero's journey we discussed in the case study structure. Even more so for the article, to increase interest and reading speed, you'll want lively quotes, active sentences, and interesting anecdotes to draw your readers' emotion. Look back at the writing chapters to review how to accomplish this.

The following structure starts you on the type of short articles we cover in this chapter. You'll use it for basic marketing styled articles rather than company profiles, new product knowledge discussions, or travel, which take slightly different structures. This article structure is meant to lead your readers toward calling you or going directly to a sale if possible. For those of you caught by the bug of writing articles, watch for my LEARN IT – DO IT book covering the structure and content of longer complex articles, proposals, and white papers.

Make a blueprint

Now we'll look at a simple way to put your thoughts in order and build the structure of your article. By this point you should know your topic, the purpose you hope to achieve in writing the article, and the audience you're directing it to. Work on structure and content just as we did with the case study template. This follows a basic story structure but is much less complex and adapts to the article you're writing.

12: Articles

Start by using a large piece of paper. I keep 11 x 17 inch paper handy for just this purpose.

- Turn it landscape and divide it into four columns.
- The first column is called the Set Up.
- At the juncture between the first and second column is the First Turning Point.
- The second column is called Development.
- At the juncture between the second and third column is the Crisis or Mid-point.
- The third column and forth columns can be separate or joined into one column depending on your story and whether or not a third turning point is used.
- The third turning point happens between the third and fourth column if you choose to use them.
- The final high point, near the end of column four, is the climax of the story if you have one. Many articles don't.
- Next, read through the descriptions that follow in Writing the Article before you fill-out your columns.
- After this, jot down in your columns (use point form) all the pieces of information you have relevant to your story. See the sidebar on using sticky notes to do this with greater flexibility for organizing your thoughts.

> **Save Time with Sticky Notes**
>
> Instead of writing your points directly on the sheet, consider using small sticky notes. Write one point on each note and stick it inside the column you've chosen.
>
> The bonus is you've not only got the flexibility to move the note to a different column, but you can arrange them in order of logical flow to make the writing task easier!

Writing the Article

Read through this section thoroughly before beginning to write! I've covered each area of the four columns and the turning points necessary to keep the reader reading.

Write a great title

The editor might change it – but he might not. Don't take a chance on being embarrassed by seeing your working title end up in print. Plus, to write a good title you must know your topic well. Encapsulating a story into one line and doing a good job of it is tough, but by doing so you've had to immerse yourself in the story. Many writers won't start the story until the title is done. It gives them a springboard to pull the writing from and can set the mood for the whole piece. Have a look at the writing section of this book for ideas on how to create a great title or headline.

Open with a hook (The set up)

Your first sentence must hook the reader, and from there each sentence does a similar job of creating interest leaving a few facts but not weighing-down the text. It must also draw the reader into the next sentence. No sentence gets a free ride. The *lead* in your article – which usually lasts a paragraph or two in a short article – is this long pull of one sentence working with the next to draw the readers in. We want to get them to a point where they've invested enough time to want to know what happens in your conclusion.

In this section, you'll build interest in your topic by lightly infusing *some* of the background information for the story. Even if your article is technical or on a serious subject, give your readers a little room to breathe as you raise the tension. If the reader doesn't need to know a point, save it until he does. This is where you set the tone and pace of your article.

12: Articles

In this part of a movie, you'd be getting to know the characters, setting, theme, and a hint of trouble to come but no heavy details. In your case study, you'd be talking about the customer and their problem.

First turning point (Between 1st & 2nd columns)
At the one quarter point of the story, you'll wake up your readers with a small turning point. A choice is made, or a character learns a piece of significant information. The story continues toward its goal, but with the new found information, the hero's (customer or main person in your article) course is changed somewhat. (And not always in the right direction.)

Talk about your customer's decision to find an answer to his challenge and as you move into the second column, discuss the ensuing misadventures – as you did with the case study, for example.

Or, if you're writing an article on the development of a product, for the turning point show where someone had an idea to make an innovative change. And in the second column show how, with each success or failure (and not too many failures for a marketing story please!), the product not only got better and better but perhaps evolved into a totally different and revolutionary product at the mid-point of the story.

Remember – this is an article on whatever topic you wish to write about. Unless you'd like to re-tell the case study completely for an e-zine, you can take your theme and the goal of your article in any direction you wish.

Mid-point (Moving into the second half)
At the mid-point or slightly further on – (known as the crisis point in fiction) – everything changes. You get the sale, or you lose the sale, you have a eureka moment in developing a prototype, or

Writing the Article

find out your customer has just shortened your lead time by a month.

Here is where the person with the innovative idea for a drug on stopping the sniffles was successful – or for a more interesting twist – was unsuccessful, but the test subject was cured of his chronic headaches. In some cases, failure *is* the high point of the story, although success comes much later, and it must be told like this.

The crisis, in story structure, doesn't necessarily indicate a crisis as we know it in life. It refers to the powerful change the character or the entity of your company for example, goes through. It sets the story up for its second half where the players take action after the crisis. The important point is – there's no turning back.

As you move into the second half of the article, you'll pick up speed. Pull out the stops and create tension and emotion in the readers. You want them in your corner as the story moves toward a conclusion so they'll be moved to act and choose your product for themselves. Include people in the anecdotes or follow one main character through the process if possible. Remember the sand in the sandwich story? (Have a look at the section on using the senses in the writing on pages 64 and 65 if you haven't yet read it.)

Time restraints also increase tension. The ticking clock works in movies and books and it works in non-fiction articles, too. Your supplier went on strike. The weather stopped the truck from arriving. The customer changed his mind about part of the solution, sending you back two weeks (when has *that* ever happened?)

Often the second half builds from the crisis point in an interesting opposite direction. If you've discovered a cure – you suddenly have problems finding a manufacturer or distributor to handle it. If your customer pulled the plug on a major installation, the buzz of the deal-breaker hit the social media network. Soon you were getting calls from companies interested in your product who'd never heard of you before.

Third turning point

Books often have a third turning point at the three-quarter mark. Short articles can use them, though room will be tight. Let's say the crisis was losing the client and you've talked about your struggle to find a new one. The three-quarter mark is where you'll bring that new client in, giving you room to adequately talk about them and what your successful sale and implementation was.

Climax

As you reach the end of the marketing article, your product should be working properly, your customer is happy, or consumers now have easy access to it. Great books and movies have one last kick at raising emotion by including a climax to the story. In short articles we don't often include it, but keep your eyes open for an interesting twist to leave readers with if you have one. Life is always stranger than fiction and it's those moments your readers truly enjoy. These personal anecdotes draw people closer to your company as an entity at the same time.

Closing the article

Recognize when it's time to close. If you've created your structure and included all the points you wanted to cover in each section – stop when you're done. If the information you're about to add is nice, but doesn't forward your original message or theme, stop. If you're hunting for more to say because you think the article isn't

Writing the Article

long enough, stop. You've written a tightly crafted, emotional roller coaster of a story and the reader is pumped and ready to call you or investigate the topic which will lead to you. Padding the ending will ruin everything you've worked for.

Keep your momentum by ending thoughtfully. This is no time to fall into clichés. Beware: At this point, you'll suddenly be hit with a wave of immense wisdom of the writing craft and know exactly how to write the ending. It will be witty and brilliant. The words will come from the ether unbidden into your head and you'll tie the opening of your story with the end in a picture perfect bundle. You hadn't planned it... it just happened. Like serendipity.

It isn't serendipity. It's predictable and clichéd. Yet I love the experience of them. I often write a neat, tied-up ending and have even submitted them to the client for approval, thinking, "This one isn't like other people's. This is a brilliant twist of word-crafting. How. Amazing. Am. I?" Thank goodness for the revision cycle because if my client doesn't stop me, usually I've had enough cooling-down time in between to stop myself. What sounds brilliant as I write it suddenly sounds trite and pedestrian. Believe me. You don't want to go there.

Try ending with a quote from a customer or answer the main question of the article if you've gone that direction with your purpose. Or end with a thought that provokes further thought on the reader's part. Lead the reader toward your company.

You'll find the perfect ending if you walk away from the article for a while and come back to it. And it won't be trite.

Real life stories can, unfortunately, be uninspiring to readers sometimes, even if the story represents a major turning point for you or your company. The key to capturing interest is in finding turning points that affect the reader. Give them what

12: Articles

they want. Include information that makes their life easier. Tell them how something will help *them* and not only how it was a success for you. Show how others benefited (such as through your case study.) Keep the WIIFM rule in mind. Raise tension, create emotion, and you'll turn prospects into customers at a greater rate.

Newsletters

If you're totally in control of the content for your printed newsletter, you can vary the length of an article however you choose. A very full 8.5 x 11 inch page article with no graphics can run as high as 575 words. With graphics and nicely spaced, I'd keep to 450 – 475 words to prevent cramping and enable the designer to include graphics and callouts for visual interest. Consider the size of the masthead or table of contents on the cover as well. These can reduce your available space by up to a third.

Half-page articles run around 225 words. The more articles you want to use, the fewer *total* number of words you'll have on the page, keeping in mind each needs a header, margins, and often a photo or illustration. Choose a clear font and widen the space between the lines to make the text easier on the reader's eyes.

If you've been asked to submit an article to a newsletter – find out how many words you've been allotted. When planning the structure, you can budget the number of sentences you have to work your way through and not be left with 20 words and half an article in content still to go.

Considering your own online newsletter?
With the cost of printing and postage on the rise – distributing a printed newsletter can be a costly venture. Many companies,

Newsletters

following the lead of most associations with even tighter budgets, have gone the electronic route.

Before you do, once again consider your readers. Do they spend a large portion of their day on the computer where they'll see your newsletter come in and possibly scan it quickly? Are you in an industry where the volume of e-mail is so overwhelming another business newsletter will scroll-up, unopened, never to be seen again? Do your readers work in retail, medical or dental offices, service stations, construction or any number of other industries where they might not open an e-mail for days?

Paper newsletters can stack-up just as quickly as the electronic ones, but there's always the chance your customer will pick up a printed copy to read over a coffee if a headline snags her attention.

One format isn't necessarily better than the other. It comes down to knowing your readers.

Making the Switch to Online Newsletters

Online Pros	Online Cons
• Inexpensive to publish	• Can be caught in spam filters
• Ability to use full color and great layouts	• High number of people won't read. Too many other e-mails vying for attention
• Easily archived and search-enabled for content	• Once "scrolled-up" – it's generally forgotten
• Rapid delivery	• People like the feel of paper in their hands

12: Articles

Aiming at Magazines and ezines

To target magazines and ezines, you first need to know their focus. Read the magazine's submission guidelines, if available, and study several past issues. (Sometimes you'll find the guidelines tucked under the contact-us tab.) As you read, you'll develop a feel for the style and tone of writing as well as the type of article the magazine likes to publish and the average number of words in each.

Also consider your audience. Every magazine caters to its own audience and we must conform to that directive.

Credibility is higher with printed magazines over ezines because rather than being self-published, articles in a magazine must be accepted by an acquisitions editor.

ezines are a popular way to place your article in the marketplace, though, and you've got much more freedom with your content in the online environment.

Keywords

When we sit down to search a topic in an Internet browser, we start with two or three words to do the search on. These are called keywords and by including them in your online articles, you increase the odds of being found.

The trick is to know which words people will choose. Don't guess. Several keyword selection tools are available to help. Google's is free, others have limited free access.

These tools enable you to find the most popular combinations of keywords, often including more specific wording that helps viewers narrow their search to you.

When you've found two or three, work them in your headlines if possible and the first paragraphs of your text in particular.

Google AdWords Keyword Tool
https://adwords.google.com/select/KeywordToolExternal

WordTracker Keywords https://freekeywords.wordtracker.com

Aiming at Magazines and ezines

If you provide sufficient forethought for including *keywords* in an online article, your story could quickly find its way climbing the search engine ranks. This is true also for your cases studies that go on your website, as well as your blog posts.

Avoiding the duplicate content trap

One thing to be aware of if targeting ezines is duplicating your articles. Google doesn't like it and prevents multiple copies of the same content (or very similar content) from being listed on their search engine. Google achieves this by checking to see which of the ezine sites you've submitted your article to, and which is getting the highest number of hits. This will be the site Google chooses to list as the source of your article.

In other words, let's say a person types-in the keywords *quiet wind turbines* and you have these words in the article you wrote. If you'd sent the same article you have on your website to a mega ezine with thousands of visitors, Google will send the person to that site and not yours. Your website listing won't even appear. In Google's eyes, the ezine is the better choice because it has the higher number of hits. This stops a multitude of duplication from appearing on the results page of a search.

The way to achieve multiple listings with your article is to send out the same article...only different. For this to work, you must revise your message substantially for each ezine. Changing a few words or rearranging the paragraphs isn't sufficient. Search engine spiders quickly recognize similar content.

On the next page, we'll have a look at one paragraph and how you can achieve keeping your message and the structure of your article intact while sending out completely different articles in the search engine's limited understanding.

12: Articles

Original Paragraph	Changed Paragraph
KVP suggested they send a logistics expert to oversee the project, put North East on track, and introduce them to the professionals at KVP who could help them going forward. The first order of business would be to send several truckloads of product to the carrier's warehouses and begin pick-and-pack operations to the surrounding box stores.	North East and KVP met to discuss options. The quickest solution was to bring one of the carrier's logistics experts to the North East facility and set up communications between the two companies. While this happened, KVP began a ten-truck shipment of product to their warehouses across the continent and immediate pick-and-pack service for the box stores.

As you can see, the wording is quite different and yet you probably felt you read the same information twice, because you did. A computer program wouldn't see it that way though, and that's the point.

How to turn your case study into an article without duplicating it word-for-word

Your marketing case study *is* a small article with a definite structure that says case study. You can increase your exposure by reworking the structure and publishing it as an ezine, blog, or printed article. This helps you avoid the online duplicate content trap (See page 127) while taking advantage of using the information you've gathered and time invested so far.

Also consider changing the focus or theme of your article. The case study can work in tandem with an article – reinforcing the message and connecting with more people of different interests. Cover as much ground as you can. Your case study has taken one specific customer challenge to solve. A spin-off article might

Aiming at Magazines and ezines

focus on the different aspects of your service – only one of them being the challenge solved in your case study.

Here are a few more article ideas for re-purposing the information you've gathered and infusing it with new points of view and specific sales objectives:

- Highlight **the case study as the focus** of an article – carefully reworded.

- Highlight the same new product or service, focusing this time on **another benefit** than you wrote about in the case study. The case study becomes peripheral but important because it shows the success of the product already.

- Highlight a **different product or service**, and reference the case study for similar points such as your successful company installation procedures or problem solving capabilities. This is your anecdotal material for gaining credibility.

- Talk about any **new industry or government initiatives** this product addresses. Take an excerpt from the case study to illustrate how it works. Find a news hook if possible. For example, perhaps you've done a case study on how your company has solved a client's cross-border shipping problems by implementing your new electronic shipping procedures. Now you want to write an article on it, but by this point the rest of the industry has already found a way to comply also so your solution doesn't hook clients as easily.

Extend your parameters. Maybe the country on the other side of the border is also initiating similar laws and the

12: Articles

scramble starts again. This time, you are ready ahead of the pack because you've implemented processes that can be easily adjusted for multiple customs' requirements, and you've purchased technology with the future in mind. Now you have a hook. While everyone else looks for a solution, your company not only has one in place but is already using it successfully.

- **Target a different reader** – for example, show the technology behind your product rather than the business solution offered in the case study. Or find a challenge in a completely **different industry sector** where customers can use your product in an entirely different way. Let's say your miniature pump for industrial applications is perfect for the swimming pool or fish pond products industry for draining water.

    Information gathered from your case study still includes great quotes for credibility and shows the product is well tested under other potentially more strenuous conditions. Always find the angle that makes your product or service look good.

- For a customer information article, **compare the product** to one of your others, showing a win-win. This form of article is great for ezines, blogs, and newsletters – but because they are obviously slanted for sales, they're unsuited for general magazines.

- **Compare your product to the competitors'**. These articles do extremely well in ezines. Be fair and honest and recognize you'll lose some sales to the competition but gain others. Recognize today's consumer is savvy and

Advertorials

hyperbole will do more harm than good. Often the best seller isn't the one with the most bells and whistles or the lowest price. If you believe in your product and use your gathered information to do it justice – you'll be well ahead of the competition.

- **Write a how-to article** that walks readers through a process using your product. Elaborate on the product's features and benefits. This structure is widely used in advertorials. It gives the readers information they can use – for free (if you can find a way) – and includes information about your product only. To make the how-to article appealing to a consumer or trade magazine, you might need to include other competing products for discussion as well.

Advertorials

Introduction to advertorials

An advertorial, just as the name implies, is a combined editorial and advertisement. You've probably read dozens, enjoying the information imparted on nutrition or finances or just about any topic. Often it's not until you reach near the end that you realize the writer has clearly mentioned a product or solution to a challenge you care about and then find the company information prominently displayed at the bottom.

Some businesses sprinkle product information liberally throughout the copy, others leave only their contact information at the bottom – using the more arms-length approach. One advertises openly the other hopes you'll want to know more and contact them without their harder sell.

People love a freebie. As a successful writer, you can learn how to give the reader free information in your advertorials

12: Articles

and articles of any kind. For example, even if you're selling vitamins enhanced to help osteoporosis, you might tell readers how calcium requires magnesium in a two-to-one ratio, how it works better when given with boron and silica, or that it should be taken in multiple doses a day rather than all at once.

Your reader might decide, "Hey, I can pick up these things at the health food store and, over time, save more money than buying this company's single product." Then when they arrive at the store, they see how your product is one easy scoop of powder over taking a half-dozen pills, and the initial outlay of cash for your one bottle is much less expensive. Plus, by now they've done a little research on the Internet and recognize how much they need your product combination to stay healthy. All-in-all your product is easier. You've met their WIIFM!

The foundation of an advertorial is much like an editorial. And although it's paid advertising, you'll do best if you stick closely to the magazine's submission guidelines for feature articles.

Because of their size, advertorials are immensely expensive. Leave nothing to chance. Research the magazine, learn about their audience by reading a few issues, and emulate their style. Your readers will flip the page from the previous story and start right into yours, enjoying the same tone and structure and absorbing the content.

Purpose of the advertorial

Long ads work. Titans of the advertising industry knew this and proved it decades ago. John Caples showed disbelievers in the 1920s by writing ads of up to four pages and stunned the companies he wrote for by making their products a household name. Along with long ads in magazines, direct mail takes the same approach through the post with the added touch of semi-personalization.

Advertorials

Advertorials take the long ad to a new level by making them noticeably un-ad-like. The marketing language is gone. The pitch is gone. Often even the product is gone. So how can they possibly sell?

They do it by creating desire. And you must too. Everything in your advertorial builds from a need the reader has and leads to one solution, coincidently, the product you offer. And if other companies offer the same thing, then your company *must* be the one readers crave to call. Anything else and your advertorial is just a paid-for story. To achieve this lure, you have to plan.

Before we get into structuring your advertorial, let's discover who will read your masterpiece and which magazine is the right choice for distribution.

Audience and magazine choice

We'll start by looking at your audience and distribution, which need to be considered at the same time. Each plays off the other.

Audience

Consider these things:
- Who are you targeting?
- What problems within this target group can you solve with your product?
- Which are the optimum publications for your target audience?

If you have the right audience in general for your company, but you're not solving their problem, your results will be less than you hoped. For example, if your company sells pool filters and heaters and you want to advertise in a tropical region, you might not want to write a story on how a heater can increase health through year-round swimming. Write about the health

12: Articles

benefits of your new super cleaning filter under sub-tropical environmental conditions instead.

Choice of Magazine

You'll also want to research the marketplace to see which magazines your target audience reads. For example, if your company manufactures outdoor fireplaces for the patio, would you write the advertorial for a high-end consumer magazine, a specialty home or pool magazine, or a trade magazine for landscapers or pool builders? If you'd like to target each, perfect! But you'll need to adapt the article for each audience group.

The easiest way to find the right publication is to ask. Ask visitors at trade shows, ask customers when you're on sales calls, ask the magazine publishers you've considered, and ask in a survey on your website. Then give it a try and see how you do. Ads – all ads – have a certain amount of hit and miss involved until you gain statistics. Advertorials are no exception.

Structuring an advertorial from a marketing perspective

An advertorial can be a few columnar inches to a four-page magazine section or a whole insert in a newspaper. The choice is yours pending how much you want to spend and the publication's space availability.

> **Mini Case Studies as Advertorials**
> Designed for insertion into newspapers, magazines, or company brochures, miniature case studies make the perfect advertorial.
>
> Create them from scratch, or cut down a current case study for two or more versions.
>
> See the case studies samples in Appendix II for an example.

Once you know how much room you have – next comes the number of photos or graphics you'll need. Color and pictures draw readers. A clean open layout also draws

Advertorials

readers. Since this is an ad, most likely you'll have a designer put it together for you just as you would for any other ad. The magazine might have restrictions on designing it to look too similar to their feature story layout, but an appealing design is important to give your advertorial a *not* ad impression.

The layout doesn't have to be complete before you write the text but a mock-up is great because you'll have a better idea exactly how many words you can use. Now you're ready to get started!

The parts of an advertorial are the same as the article we did in the last chapter. The differences are you're allowed to promote your company in an advertorial and you're not looked down upon if you don't include every little pro and con – mostly cons. On the other hand – keep the content absolutely accurate and never mislead your readers.

Ensure you know the audience's need – the problem your product remedies – and place it front and center in your lead paragraphs. This is all about what the customer wants from you and you can supply, and not what you want to tell them.

Make the story lively and interesting to keep your readers' attention, but above all, keep the information true and verifiable. Build your potential customer's confidence.

Use great quotes from your case study or interview (with permission) and touch on the case study to build credibility. Review the basics on article writing and you're ready to get started.

13: Blogs

Draw traffic to your website and case studies through the powerful, and often under-used blog. What started several years ago as an online diary, blogs are now a *must* for companies and individuals marketing their services.

Raise your company's visibility – Blogs are "crawled" by spiders (nasty but good!) and picked up by the search engine giants. Blog posts are often listed among the top web pages on a search engine's landing page. With blog directory giants such as Technorati, you can additionally register your blog so they'll start monitoring it right away.

The more frequently you update your blog, and the more care you take in choice of key words (See page 126), the better the chance your blog will shoot-up the page rank.

The Purpose of Using a Blog in Your Marketing

Increasing your scope of potential customers (Visibility) – The blog brings people to meet you in an informal atmosphere. Maybe they first met you on Twitter or in the comment section of someone else's post or in a search. They followed the link to your blog because they saw something they liked.

13: Blogs

Keep the friendly atmosphere going with informative posts that serve a need the visitor has. Add short editorials and view points to start conversations going. Your blog could become *the* place to visit for industry professionals.

Create the Atmosphere

Think of your blog as a comfortable online sitting room where everyone can visit, read, and chat in an informal atmosphere. It's not your office. Your website is your office. Through your blog you hope to entice readers to click the visible but not irritatingly intrusive links to your website when they're ready or to sign up for a newsletter or other giveaway by going though your opt-in form. (See page 111.)

On the blog, give readers appetizers of free information (which might be all they want at the moment) – but leave the door open to your full menu on the website or through other means.

- Introduce a great idea that solves a problem (which also happens to mesh with your latest product launch.) Provide links to more free information in the form of a case study or white paper.
- Make people realize they need your service.
- Lead them to your website to buy it.

Most importantly, keep your posts regular to build a returning audience. The more people who know and trust you, the greater your chances they'll take the next step toward becoming a customer. Here are a few ideas on how to do it:

Current information updates – Everyone likes to be first. First to see the latest movie, first to own the latest mobile phone, and first to have your product or service. Or that's the way you

Create the Atmosphere

want people to think of your company products. A blog is the perfect place to tell readers your hot-off-the-press details – without selling.

You've given them the first exclusive look of a product and perhaps – if you're a good marketer – you'll give them a tangible reward for being a loyal reader. Keep them coming back and when they buy – reward them for it.

Credibility – Just as the case study puts real people behind your products, a blog puts *you* out there to meet your prospects. This is your chance to show genuine interest in helping people without being perceived as selling. Offer plenty of customer service through this venue. If you have a team of writers for your company blog – make sure you or the boss have a say from time-to-time. Huge corporations and top politicians know the value in using this valuable tool to connect with their readers. Your company should too.

Credibility also comes from third party opinions, as we've discussed already. This is where case study material and customer quotes come into play and where a guest interview can give your product a boost.

Feedback – The comments feature on a blog is entirely optional but incredibly useful. It's not just a place to let readers have their say – it's your way into letting them talk directly to you, the owner, or CEO, and see *immediate* results through your response. They witness your company listening to its customers and acting on their issues. Few things gain loyalty like personal service and a feeling of importance.

Staying open minded through this process is vital – as is responding quickly to blog comments. Feedback through the blog is an entirely free and unsolicited opinion of your company by a cross-section of your target audience. Whereas participants in focus groups can be shy to speak up and haven't had the opportunity to use the product in question in their homes, blog respondents have taken the time to form an opinion (hopefully one with constructive criticism if not glowing remarks) and go to you with it.

Most blog programs allow you to enable or disable comments, and if enabled, choose the option of approving comments before they're posted. You can always delete any unfair posts but allow a few that don't glow as highly as you'd like. You'll increase your credibility and make your company look good when you (a) respond to the comment and (b) if applicable, correct the issue or make changes so others with the same point of view will know why it is as it is.

Audience

Aim at the same audience you do with your website, but give more information away. You never know who found your blog article from a search engine query and stayed to look around. Provide a little variety and appeal for people who aren't familiar with your business. They could always open up a brand new channel of distribution you haven't thought of before.

Structure – From a Marketing Perspective

Blogs started their lives as journals that went wired and it's one vehicle where almost anything goes. Write, add photos, add video, invite comments or guest writers – or enjoy working through ideas with your readers' feedback. For companies, these few guidelines help too:

- Blogs are not meant for selling. Readers go to a blog to find updates on your business, connect with you, and get

Structure – From a Marketing Perspective

free information...so they don't have to buy it. Give them enough information to accomplish what they need on some things and keep them coming back for more, until one day you don't provide everything they need but they trust you enough to buy.

- Keep the content short. Though once in a while you might want to include a long post, most should stay under 250 words. People are attracted to short bursts of writing. Plus, you want the reader to go to your website where you are able to sell. Give the reader short bursts of useful information on the blog and emphasize the more complete – and equally free – content on your website or better, sent by e-mail.
- Include an opt-in form. (See page 111.) Blogs provide a perfect source of new contacts for your marketing list. Readers should always pass through the opt-in form before anything is sent.
- Offer to send semi-regular communications such as newsletters or eblasts to notify people of a product launch or new blog post.
- Get to the point quickly. People have little time to wade through information to find your message. If they don't find it quickly, they'll pass and move on. Put your point visibly in the title or subtitle, or certainly within the first couple of sentences. One method of advertising that doesn't work as well today as it did in the past is curiosity. Once upon a time you could tease readers into continuing with a promise of rewards later. Now they want to know what you're talking about right away and decide if they'll invest the time to read more.

13: Blogs

- Use keywords in your blogs, just as you do in ezines. (See page 126.)

Advertising

All this talk of not selling might lead you to the idea you can't discuss your product at all. It's true, you don't want to sell in your posts. You certainly *can* lead readers to a line or two in a sidebar on the product you've developed that coincides with the post. Link from there to your website.

The blogs we're drawn to most often don't mix sales in with their posts, but keep offers to the side or the bottom areas of the blog for readers to choose, or not, to look at.

Blogs are also used extensively as a revenue stream for other people's products. You can sell space or sign-up with companies such as Google AdSense. Be aware you generally do not have control over what ad will appear on your site at any given moment if you go that route. Not all blogs are suited for this, but in many cases the ads complement what your company's strengths are. You need to gauge the level of commercialism you want to include and build your blog accordingly.

http://www.google.com/ads/

Using Your Case Study Material in a Blog

Your case study is a natural fit for a blog. It has action, suspense, third party quotes that sell your business, and it also comes with plenty of information for interested customer prospects. Much as you read in chapter 11 on eblasts, you'll use the opening of the case study to hook readers and the offer of the free downloadable case study to invite them one step closer. You can do this two ways:

- Introduce the case study in a couple of lines on the blog and link it to your website. You want readers to take the next step toward the sale. You'll get more visitors to your site but will not retain any customer information unless they contact you.
- To capture the e-mail address, you would paste-in the opening of the case study or write a short overview about it to hook the reader. Then provide an opt-in form, or a link to one, to secure the reader's e-mail address and have your auto responder company forward the case study immediately.

Keeping the Content Fresh

Free information is the lifeblood of the Internet. It's the first place we look if we don't have a reference book handy…and sometimes even if we do. We expect if we look hard enough, and intelligently sift through the rubble out there, we can find anything we want.

Your company has the opportunity to be one of those sources and capture your reader's attention through your articles and blog. Keep your content fresh and you'll additionally raise your position on the search engines' pages as a good landing page for its customers.

As a wrap-up to not only the blogs chapter but also for eblasts and articles, I'd like you to keep these next few points in mind to help keep your marketing materials fresh and interesting.

- **Don't save it.** From fiction to advertising to writing a blog post, we're always analyzing how worthy the reader is for our pearls of wisdom and if, possibly, we should hold onto our best ideas for later. Every writer does

13: Blogs

it. But unless you have the actual document in mind you're saving a juicy morsel of information for, use it now. Chances are the exact right opportunity to use your special turn of phrase won't come up again, and your mind gave it to you today to use in the work you're doing today. So use it.

- **What happens when topics are thin?** Avoid writing dull posts no matter how desperate your landscape of ideas. If you're not interested in a topic – no one else will be either. Put a plan in place so you're never down to the wire with no ideas. Keep at least a month's worth on your list...which might be only four...and while researching them, look for ways to branch out for further articles.

  - Consider working with other people in your industry and *guesting* for each other. For example, if you own a training facility for horseback riding and you run out of tips to share with riders, consider joining forces with a saddle-making facility and post articles on saddle fitting, too. Or ask a veterinarian to post comments on caring for a horse. Or give readers creative ideas on how to find local trails and historical sites. You can write articles posted elsewhere by others (with permission), or *ask them to join you in a chat-type forum* where readers will get a better sense of their thoughts on your company and products through discussion.

  - If your company is large enough, set up a schedule for each major department in your company where each must supply a post monthly. Remind them the

In Conclusion

post has to be of interest to your audience or you'll be back to the dull post syndrome again.
- Free articles are also available on the Internet. Enter *free blog articles* or similar search words into your preferred search engine and you'll find dozens of directories.
- Use Google Alerts to watch for topics relevant to your business. You can search on them manually (much like using the search engine itself.) Or set up parameters for Google to check your key words at particular intervals, and within certain criteria such as Everything, News, Blogs, Realtime, Video, and Discussion. You can then enter your e-mail address and Google alerts you when it gets a hit.

  Google Alerts are perfect for spotting news hooks for press releases as well.

  http://www.google.com/alerts
- Over all, keep a fresh list of case studies, white papers, and even contest ideas handy to bring blog readers to your website.

In Conclusion

Why does a professionally written case study, article or report read so well and seemingly connect all the points you wanted into a logical flow and persuasive argument? Is there a magic bullet you can use to write one, too?

Training yourself, practicing what you've learned, and time spent polishing in the revision cycle are crucial. But paramount to any document is the underlying structure and purpose for

13: Blogs

choosing each form – the case study or the article – the e-mail or the eblast.

Until you know your goals for your documents, and until you lay out all your material into a logical flow, your finished pieces won't entice anyone to buy. But with this structure behind you, you'll have all you need to create persuasive materials for your next marketing campaign. Answer the questions your readers want to know and make it easy for them to succeed. WIIFM!

Enjoy yourself in the process!

Appendix I – A Word on Testimonials

Used on your website, in brochures, on book covers, or as callouts in articles, testimonials are a staple part of your everyday marketing plan. We all want them – but for the most part we all hate asking for them. If you have a case study in hand already, your customer is obviously pleased with your company's services. While they're working with you on the study, take the process a step further and ask if you can also quote them for a testimonial.

Often they'll ask you to put something together and they'll okay it – but it's difficult to write a glowing recommendation about your own company and expect someone else to put their name to it. Plus, you'll end up with a list of testimonials that sound surprisingly alike despite your best efforts to make them sound different.

Fortunately, once again you're ahead of the pack. One of the best places to find candid testimonial statements is in your case study interview transcript. Under normal circumstances when asked to write a testimonial, a client is so careful of putting the right works together for you, he'll squeeze the life from the statement. During a conversation, however, dialogue is free and casual. The testimonial comes from the heart and the reader can tell. Your transcript is filled with just this kind of language.

Appendix I – A Word on Testimonials

You've probably already taken the best quotes for your case study and you can use them again along with a few extra words to put the quote in context. But search a little harder in your interview transcript to where the conversation is moving along pleasantly and you'll also find interesting nuggets that don't quite make a full sentence or fit within your idea for a fascinating testimonial.

Now, cobble these bits from here and there and see what you have. Have a look at page 62 where we worked on developing a quote. It's the same idea.

Keep the flavor of the client's voice, so the writing doesn't sound like you, but refrain from quoting word-for-word. Everyday speech abounds with filler words as we put thoughts together, repeat ideas, and choose words we would much rather have polished than used straight for a quote. Do your best to make your contact sound good, and send it along for review.

The testimonial *must* be approved by the client, and what he'll find are a collection of his words or ideas that usually need only a little tweaking. Sometimes your made-up quotes make it through on the first go, but human nature being what it is, your interviewee will usually change a few words or provide the perfect quote you wanted in the first place. Often people just need a draft in hand to provide them the inspiration for a marvelous quotable testimonial.

Appendix II: Case Study Samples

The following case studies provide samples of what we have discussed throughout the book.

- I've provided three longer length case studies, which give you an idea of the word-count you might arrive at in your first draft or if you're looking for two pages. These are perfect for sending-out when a prospect or a customer requests one. The additional information provides extra value in these situations. They also work for double-sided handouts and on your website if you feel it's important to thoroughly explain points. Remember to follow the Ten Tips for Strengthening Your Writing.
- Following these case studies are a few pointers on cutting a case study (or any article) down in size while retaining the structure and pertinent points. I've included a table showing the process.
- The last sample is the same case study revised heavily to a miniature size for brochures or small advertorials.

I've reused the transportation case study, for comparison purposes, among the three lengths.

… Appendix II: Case Study Samples

Case Study Samples

The this first sample, I've used descriptive headers which could be skimmed by the reader for an overview of the story. The second uses the standard headings of a case study, and the third uses no headings at all, leaving the reader with a story but no markers if he merely glanced at it. As you read each, you'll have a better sense of which format works best for you.

KVP Helps Secure Big Box Store Contract
Innovative Solutions During Crisis Ensures North American Big Box Deliveries Stay on Schedule

North East Paper Products is an Ohio-based mid-sized manufacturer of household paper towels, bathroom tissue, and industrial wipes.

When labor issues at a competing supplier of these products led a major North American box store to research new interim and potentially permanent suppliers, they gave North East a chance in mid-June.

The Scramble to Find Transportation

Even with facilities in the east and western United States, with their suddenly huge new territory to cover, including cross-border delivery to Canada, North East's shipping became an urgent challenge. This task was made more difficult by the increasing capacity issues within a diminished trucking industry. Transportation costs were also an issue with the high volume

Case Study Samples

but low profit margin on paper products. North East decided to handle their shipping with a third-party broker that would find the least expensive transportation for each facility's region.

Then disaster struck. North East's larger west coast facility went offline when a fire ravaged the building the first week of July. This forced the eastern facility to fill orders across the continent and maintain deliveries on time. The box store had a fixed rule on out-of-stocks – three times and the vendor is released.

Meanwhile, supplying to the western stores under such a tight schedule was almost impossible. By the third shipping week after the fire, North East had incurred their first delivery non-compliance and their carriers were charging them back for long wait-times at the stores' docks. The only carrier that consistently did well was KVP Carrier from the Chicago region.

On Board with KVP Carrier

With North East's reliable but local company unable to help them and the third party broker giving them mixed results, they needed a better solution. They researched KVP and learned its head office was in Illinois and they had warehousing facilities and truck terminals in six additional centers in the US and Canada. Plus they had recently set up an intermodal partnership with two rail lines. They also had in-house customs services, electronic customs submissions, and satellite tracking. This was ideal for North East's shipping department, which was now clearly overwhelmed and unprepared for their new rigorous requirements.

KVP suggested sending a logistics expert to oversee the project, put North East on track, and introduce them to professionals who could help them going forward. The first order of business would be to send several truckloads of product to the carrier's warehouses and begin pick-and-pack operations to the surrounding box stores.

Avoiding Disaster

"Just as product began moving and we'd started to relax, disaster struck again with the onset of August's flash floods in the central USA," said Peter Murray, Director of Logistics for North East. "Two main highways to the west were closed, but KVP came through once more."

Because they continually schedule lanes of traffic across the continent, they were already prepared with an alternate solution. They put their intermodal service into effect immediately and included North East's products in their rail shipments. The freight went to the KVP western terminals where their trucks moved it to their warehouses and straight to the stores.

First Class Results

Although rail was the more expensive option for general shipping, using it during the emergency made the difference by saving the big box contract.

"KVP's operations and transportation managers are first class," said Murray. "They knew what we needed before we did and were proactive, recognizing our time restraints and putting a solution into place."

North East's western facility was running again by September, but KVP still transports all their shipments. "They came through for us in a crisis," said Murray. "Since then our on-time delivery rate has increased to 98%. We've kept our shipping costs to the client stable, and we track our freight real time throughout the continent. Why would we trust anyone else?"

Case Study Samples

This second example uses standard case study headings. As another variation for you to see, I've also used the first person, I, in recounting the story. I would change this to my name or company if I rewrote for any other vehicle than my website or blog:

Writing Coach Helps Secure Publishing Deal
Jack K. Supports Editing Assistance for Writers in Highly Competitive Publishing Industry

The Challenge

Author Jack K. had more than one hundred short stories to his credit but hadn't been successful at breaking into book-length fiction. He was comfortable with the shorter word-length and developed compelling tales his readers loved. His longer work didn't do as well. Editors rejected his latest novel as lacking emotional depth as a result of poor character development and a one-dimensional plot.

Jack was accomplished at telling stories but needed to understand the structure and breadth of a novel and the techniques available to develop characters readers could empathize with. He had the technical skills and experience to write well and the knowledge to expand his ideas into a novel but couldn't actualize what he knew and write a manuscript editors wanted. Yet, he was reticent to ask for help.

Jack's challenge was to overcome his resistance to being coached. To him, being coached was synonymous with having his style leeched and replaced with a set of rules. Additionally, he had his novel already completed and wasn't interested in going through a lengthy work-in-progress program.

Appendix II: Case Study Samples

Our Approach

Jack was referred to me by an author I regularly work with and he was hesitant in his call. I asked Jack to send me his book synopsis and the first three chapters for evaluation. The problem was apparent immediately. Because he'd mastered the short story, he was used to tying-up loose ends and solving the conflict within that limited word count...a comparable word count to a chapter in a novel. We needed to reverse that trend and throw more conflict at his hero at each chapter's conclusion so readers would turn the page instead of closing the book for the night.

Jack's editor agreed with the solution but wasn't convinced this alone was enough to bring Jack's character and dilemma alive on the page. The crisis wasn't sufficiently compelling.

After studying the turning points and how much the character had to lose at the crisis moment, we spotted an opening. By devising a sub-plot for one of his secondary characters, Jack could intertwine a new set of problems with the main character's original ones, giving the plot more depth because the sacrifice to the character was greater.

We achieved this through several one-to-one lessons, targeting different points and stages of the book in each. Jack quickly grasped the dynamics of infusing more emotional depth into his writing. Because he'd stopped solving each chapter crisis, he also gained room to grow the overall tension. Within a few meetings, he was able to halt our coaching and continue with the rewrites on his own.

The Result

As a result of his efforts, Jack was awarded a contract after minimal further changes by the publisher. He is currently plotting a new book for the secondary character in this first one.

Case Study Samples

Professional writers face a frustrating dilemma once they reach a certain plateau. They have fewer avenues to advance their craft. Many courses are taught by writers with less experience or widely differing approaches. At Paula Wheeler Creative Studios, beginners and novices find the instruction they need based on the skills they bring to the table, and they can leave at any time they feel confident to carry on with what they've learned.

"Paula took one look at my manuscript and instantly saw what the editors saw," said Jack K. "Even better, she enabled me to understand the story structure so I can bring this new skill with me to my next novel. I encourage new writers or authors changing genres to reduce their learning curve through Paula's one-to-one coaching."

• •

In this next sample, I've removed the headings and added a few bullet points to break up the text. Notice the difference between this and the first sample where you knew where you were in the story simply by glancing at the subheads.

KVP Solves Remote-Access Security Issue
Restaurant Chain Receives 24/7 System in Internet-Deficient Region

With a rapidly expanding chain of fast food diners to oversee, owner of Plucki Chicken Fritters, Don Wyatt, had his hands full. The company now covered two states and Wyatt found he couldn't maintain his weekly visit to each site. Without the visits, he felt less in control and worried security and quality might slip.

- Turnover wasn't high, but good managers were hard to find and covering all shifts was difficult. Without proper

Appendix II: Case Study Samples

leadership on the late shift, the building's security could be at risk if night lock-down procedures weren't followed.

- Utility expenses had slowly increased as well and with winter approaching Wyatt wanted control over the thermostats, especially if someone forgot to turn them down at night.
- Added to these worries, federal regulations were strict. New employees had been known to leave a freezer door ajar by accident when rushing to carry out their tasks.

He investigated remote monitoring as a first step at keeping the restaurants up to standards.

Wyatt first went to alarm companies. This would provide him with basic building safety. Next came the utilities. He found one company that monitored temperature but reports were generated 24 hours later. A second company offered real-time reporting but was expensive for ten locations. They additionally regulated freezer temperatures as requested.

Before making a decision, he went to an energy seminar put on by his local Chamber of Commerce and came across KVP Energy Corp.

KVP specializes in offering energy services to small sized groups such as the Plucki Chicken Fritters chain. Once they'd reviewed Wyatt's request, they customized a solution to cover all three areas Wyatt identified plus additional features. They offered him remote access to the temperature controls of his freezers and the climate control of his building. They would also install small alarms to notify employees if a freezer door was left ajar for more than a pre-set time limit.

"We tested two locations first with a complete roll-out scheduled for December," Wyatt explained. "Timing would be tight, but I wanted to have everything in place before the winter break at school when the restaurants would run at full capacity. KVP assured me they could do it."

The installations went smoothly, with KVP's technicians arriving well before business hours with new computer hardware and cables and finishing just as the doors opened each day. Two days later they were ready to test.

Fortunately, they were alerted to a problem right away. One of the two restaurants was in a smaller community which had no access to the suggested always-on broadband Internet service. Regular cable service and DSL wasn't available in this region. At least three other locations in the chain would have similar problems.

KVP developed a workaround but it would set the project back a few days until new third party Internet hardware and service was installed, but the results were perfect. The roll-out installation schedule was tightened-up and the project completed before school broke for the holidays.

"We've been operating with KVP's service for three months now, the coldest time of the year, and heating costs are down by 20% over last year," Wyatt added. "Of all the features this solution has provided, though, the remote access to environmental heat and the freezers' thermostats has given me the greatest peace of mind. I can control a freezer's temperature with a simple adjustment at my home computer. If the monitor still reads too high a few minutes later, I know there's a problem and will send the manager back in. It's happened only once when the thermostat on one freezer didn't react properly after a power interruption. Knowing I had the problem, not being able to rectify it myself, and having a great manager to rely on, meant we didn't lose several hundred dollars in food product.

"Now... if KVP could find a way to outfit my whole chain with great managers as well, I'd be really happy!"

Appendix II: Case Study Samples

Shortening Your Case Study

Even if you find you need two or three pages to properly develop your case study, you might consider saving it for giveaways and using a shorter one page version in your website, ezine ariticles, and handouts.

Stick to your structure to ensure all the relevant information makes the cut and to understand how to do this without sacrificing the flow of logic or readability.

Start by marking all the important information for each section. Don't be concerned about the sentence structure at this point – you'll need to recast sentences anyway to make the new case study flow better. Refer to your template if you have it handy or follow the one in this book. Identify areas such as the customer, what their business does, the challenge, what they did to rectify the problem before coming to you... all the main points you worked through to build the case study. By doing this, you won't miss any critical information.

If you like working on paper, print the original case study and use a pencil or highlighter to mark the main points.

If you prefer working on the computer – I'd suggest while you're getting the knack of this, you could try setting up a two-column table in your word processing software and pasting the original case study into the first column. Bold or highlight the same information as mentioned above so you can see what you'll be working with. In the other column, write your new text.

For this example I've bolded the text for easier legibility in print. Here's the transportation case study cut down by nearly 300 words:

Shortening Your Case Study

Longer version

KVP Helps Secure Big Box Contract

Innovative Solutions During Crisis Ensures North American Big Box Deliveries Stay on Schedule

North East Paper Products is an Ohio-based mid-sized manufacturer of household paper towels, bathroom tissue, and industrial wipes.

When labor issues at a competing supplier of these products led a major North American box store to research new interim and potentially permanent suppliers, they gave North East a chance in mid-June.

The Scramble to Find Transportation

Even with facilities in the east and western states, with their suddenly huge new territory to cover, including cross-border delivery

Shorter version

KVP Helps Secure Big Box Contract

Innovative Solutions During Crisis Ensures North American Big Box Deliveries Stay on Schedule

North East Paper Products is an Ohio-based manufacturer of household and industrial tissues and wipes.

In June, when labor issues at a competing supplier led a major North American box store to look for alternative suppliers, they gave North East a chance.

The Scramble to Find Transportation

Even with facilities in the east and west, the new expanded US and Canadian territory made shipping an urgent challenge.

Appendix II: Case Study Samples

to Canada, North East's **shipping became an urgent challenge.** This task was made more difficult by the increasing capacity issues within a diminished trucking industry. With the **high volume but low profit margin on paper products, cost was also an issue.** North East decided to handle their **shipping with a third-party broker, who would find the least expensive available transportation** for each facility's region.

Then disaster struck. North East's **larger west coast facility went offline when a fire ravaged the building the first week of July. This forced the eastern facility to fill orders across the continent and maintain deliveries on time.** The box store had a fixed rule on **out-of-stocks – three times and the vendor is released**.

Meanwhile, supplying to the western stores under such a tight schedule was almost impossible. By the third ship-

North East's product was high volume but low profit margin, making shipping costs a significant issue.

They decided to choose a third-party broker who could do the leg work for them and handle the day-to-day paperwork.

Then disaster struck. North East's larger west coast facility went offline when a fire ravaged the building the first week of July. This forced the eastern facility to fill orders across the continent and maintain deliveries on time. The box store had a fixed rule on out-of-stocks – three times and the vendor is released.

With the tight schedule and sporadic success with freight

Shortening Your Case Study

ping week after the fire, **North East had incurred their first delivery non-compliance** and their carriers were charging them back for long wait-times at the stores' docks. **The only carrier that consistently did well was KVP Carrier from the Chicago region.**

On Board with KVP Carrier

With North East's reliable but local company unable to help them and the third party broker giving them mixed results, they needed a better solution. **They researched KVP** and learned its head office was in Illinois and they had **warehousing facilities and truck terminals in six additional centers in the US and Canada. Plus they had recently set up an intermodal partnership with two rail lines.** They also had in-house **customs services, electronic customs submissions, and satellite tracking.** This was ideal for North East's shipping department, which was **now**

companies, North East had earned its first non-compliance penalty three weeks later.

Only KVP Carrier, from the Chicago region, provided consistently strong service.

On Board with KVP Carrier

Exactly the carrier North East needed, KVP offered full service warehousing facilities, six terminals across the US and Canada, ties with two rail lines, inside custom services, electronic customs submissions, and satellite tracking in all their trucks.

For the overwhelmed manufacturer, this was perfect.

Appendix II: Case Study Samples

clearly overwhelmed and unprepared for their new rigorous requirements.

KVP suggested sending a logistics expert to oversee the project, put North East on track, and introduce them to professionals who could help them going forward. The **first order of business would be to send several truckloads of product to the carrier's warehouses and begin pick-and-pack operations to the surrounding box stores.**

Avoiding Disaster

"**Just as product began moving and we'd started to relax, disaster struck again with the onset of August's flash floods in the central USA,**" said Peter Murray, Director of Logistics for North East. "**Two main highways to the west were closed. But KVP came through once more.**"

Because they continually schedule lanes of traffic across KVP sent a logistics expert, who prepared several truckloads of product to their warehouses and immediately began pick-and-pack operations to the surrounding box stores.

Avoiding Disaster

"Just as product began moving and we'd started to relax, disaster struck again with the onset of August's flash floods in the central USA," said Peter Murray, Director of Logistics for North East. "Two main highways to the west were closed. But KVP came through once more."

They included North East's products with their current rail shipments to the west, where their trucks took the product to their warehouses and straight to the stores.

Shortening Your Case Study

the continent, they were already prepared with an alternate solution. They put their intermodal service into effect immediately and **included North East's products in their rail shipments.** The freight went to the KVP **western terminals where their trucks moved it to their warehouses and straight to the stores.**

First Class Results

Although rail was the more expensive option for general shipping, using it during the emergency made the difference by saving the big box contract.

"KVP's operations and transportation managers are first class," said Murray. **"They knew what we needed before we did and were proactive, recognizing our time restraints and putting a solution into place."**

North East's western facility was running again

First Class Results

Though rail was a more expensive method, in the emergency it saved North East its contract.

Appendix II: Case Study Samples

by September, but KVP still transports all North East's shipments. "They came through for us in a crisis," said Murray. "**Since then our on-time delivery rate has increased to 98%. We've kept our shipping costs to the client stable, and we track our freight real time throughout the continent.** Why would we trust anyone else?"

"KVP knew what we needed before we did and were proactive, recognizing our time restraints and putting a solution into place," said Murray.

"Since then our on-time delivery rate has increased to 98%. We've kept our shipping costs to the client stable, and we track our freight real time throughout the continent. Why would we trust anyone else?"

Switching to Advertising Language

With another pass, we could take the case study down even further and still retain the integrity of the structure. At this point we'd begin sacrificing specifics to enable us to smoothly condense whole sections into a couple of paragraphs, but as long as the structure was intact, the message would flow logically.

Next we'll take this same study and while I let you reduce it further if you wish on your own, I'll give you an example of miniaturizing it for a magazine ad or the back of a handout or brochure.

Watch for the same structural elements of the company and the challenge, approach, implementation, and results.

Switching to Advertising Language

Because we're moving away from the tone of an article by creating these miniature case studies as ads or marketing pieces, we can make the language even lighter and more sales driven. The exception would be if your audience is less consumer-based and they'd appreciate a more technical or scientific tone with solid information.

- These small case studies range from approximately 150 to 300 words pending the size of space you have.
- Keep graphics in mind as well and work with your designer to achieve a balance.
- Include quotations and bullet points, as needed, to keep the content open and appealing to the eye. Bullets also let you include more information into a smaller space – as long as you don't overdo them so readers skim past.

Appendix II: Case Study Samples

Transportation Carrier's Innovation Saves Big Box Account

When one of the nation's largest box stores came calling, Peter Murray of North East Paper Products was ready. "We were just building momentum when a fire in our western facility put a halt to production and an overwhelming strain on our smaller eastern plant," he said.

The company rallied the staff to meet production needs, but shipping problems became critical. "Within three weeks we were hit by compliance fines," said Murray, who realized without a solution, they'd lose their contract with the retailer.

Fortunately, through the third-party truck broker they'd tried, KVP Carrier made several deliveries for them.

"They sent us logistics experts to help when we approached them directly with our problem," said Murray.

With a solution prepared for the high-volume low-cost paper towel products North East produced, KVP soon had shipments on the road to their warehouses and terminals across North America.

"I would have been grateful even with this – but that's not the end of the story," Murray explained. "Flooding closed roads to the west and KVP found space for us among their rail car freight. We didn't miss a single deadline."

With KVP on board, North East has maintained their shipping costs and reached a 98% on-time delivery rate. "Why would we trust anyone else?"

Index

A

Advertorials 131–135, 165. *See also* Articles
  audience 133–134
  magazine choice 133–134
  magazine guidelines 132
  paid advertising 132
  promote 135
  purpose of 132
Articles 115–135
  blueprint 117–118
  closing 122–124
  duplicate content 127
  multiple listings 127
  re-purposed 129–131
  structuring 117
  title 119. *See also* Headlines and Subheads
  turning points 120–122
  writing 119
Audience 20, 66, 116
  business 20
  consumer 20

B

Blogs 137–145
  advertising 142
  audience 140
  case study material 142
  content updates 143
  credibility 139
  feedback 139–140
  information updates 138
  marketing 137
  posting regularly 138
  purpose 137–138
  search engine 137
  selling 142
  spiders 137
  trust, building 138–140
Build a list 110–111
  opt-in forms 111

C

Case studies
  ad language 165
  definition 13
  getting to yes 23–24
  Mini case studies 134
  multiple 23
  timing 22
  where to use 14–16
  why use 13
Case study samples 149
Clients
  finding 22–24
  scheduling 24
Copywriter. *See* Writers; Writing
Credibility 13–14, 36, 38, 47, 94, 106, 115, 126, 139
Customer Sign-Off 16, 48

E

eblasts 109–114
  build a list 110
  case study, in 114
  contest forms 110
  opt-in form 111–112
  personalizing 110, 113–114
  sign-up book 110

Index

solicited 109
spam 109
unsolicited 109
unsubscribing 112
why use them? 109
Editing 75–89
  active / passive 78–79
  and/but, begin a sentence with 86
  faulty parallelism 84
  first pass 76–77
  it is / there are 81
  modifiers 82–83
  one contact 75
  preposition, end a sentence with 87
  problems with revisions 76
  repetition, redundancy, and padding 84–85
  revision cycle 75–77
  split infinitives 86
  strengthen your writing 77
  subject-verb agreement 80
  Ten Tips for Strengthening Your Writing 78
  that 82
  unclear antecedents 83
  verb choice 79–80
  WIIFM (what's in it for me) 85
e-mails. *See* eblasts
ezines 126–131

G

Google 127
Google AdSense 142
Google Alerts 145

H

Handouts
  case study 93–94
Headlines and Subheads 68–73, 104
  descriptive 69
  headline 30
  skimmers 68–69
  snapshot view 69
  tips 70–73
  traditional, for case studies 69
  typography 72
  WIIFM. *See* WIIFM (What's in it for me?)

I

Interview 47–55
  ending the call 53–54
  making the call 50–54
  numbers sell 52
  personal perspective 52
  preparation 49
  tricks 51–52

K

Keywords 69, 126, 127

L

Lists
  opt-in forms 111
  solicited 110
  unsolicited 110
  unsubscribing 112

M

Magazines 126–131
Media releases 95–108
　backgrounder 108
　contact information 97
　credibility 97–98
　editor, attracting attention 95
　ending 107
　fact sheet 108
　focus 100
　format 101
　goal 99
　header 102–103
　headline and subheads 104
　quotes 106–107
　readers, holding attention 96
　reverse pyramid 104–106
　sales 98–99
　visibility 96–97
　why write them? 96

N

News hook 32, 103, 145. *See also* Media releases
Newsletters 124–130. *See* Articles
　length 124
　number of words 124
　printed 124
　reader availability, online 125

O

Opt-in forms 111–112, 143
　auto responders 111
　AWeber 111

P

People
　include 35, 37
Photos 94
Point Form 58
Polish Your Prose. *See* Editing
Press releases. *See* Media releases

Q

Quotations 59–62, 106
　handling 60–61
　journalists vs. business writers 61
　use of names 107

R

Readers. *See* Audience
Recording Equipment 53
Research 25, 59

S

SEO
　definition 19
Sign off, customer 16, 46
Specifics, used in writing 32, 37, 72
　results, case study 38–39, 51
　sales power, for 63
Structure, Case study 27–38
　approach 33–34
　basic structure 27
　challenge 32
　classic story structure 27
　compare to books, articles, movies 28

Index

customer 30–32
discovery point 34
hero 28
implementation 36
installation. *See* Implementation
quest. *See* Approach
raise interest 29
results 38–39
solution 35–37
tension, importance of 36

T

Technical information
  jargon 16
Template, Case study 41–46
  background information 43
  challenge 43–44
  closing 46
  customer 43
  customer information 42
  download a copy www.learnit-doit.com/cstemp10.html 46
  implementation 45
  interview, for 42
  quest (approach) 44
  results 45–46
  solution 45
  structure, for 42
Tension 29, 35, 36, 121
Testimonials 16, 147
Tone 28
Topics 22–23
Transcript 54–55
  quotes 55
Typography
  font 101
  headlines 72

W

WIIFM (What's in it for me?) 31, 70, 85, 94
Word Choice, see also Specifics 63
Writers
  experts 21
  non-experts 21
  (SME) subject matter expert.
Writing
  company style 22
  consumer 20
  editing 16
  emotion, raising 64, 121, 122
  first words 67
  hook 119
  lead 119
  padding 64
  planning ahead 16
  preparation 57–66
  specifics, use of. *See* Specifics, used in writing
  story telling 20
  strengthen 77
  tightening 64
  tricks 16–17
  useability testing 21

About the Author

Paula Wheeler has been a writer and editor for business and industry since 1998. She specializes in developing sales guides and consumer user guides, bridging the information gap between the subject matter expert and the reader. She now works with other authors in fiction and non-fiction as well as publishing her latest series of books. She resides north of Toronto, Canada with her husband Les. (Who never complained when it was frozen pizza night...again...as this book was in the final stages. Thank you!)

The *Learn It – Do It* book series is designed to give readers the theory and practical information needed to get up and running in their chosen topic. Watch for upcoming titles on a variety of subjects such as writing your own advertising and writing your own longer documents.

For more information on the series or to contact Paula, please visit:

www.learnit-doit.com

and

www.knight-vision.com

To download a copy of the Case Study template and Ten Tips for Strengthening Your Writing, please visit:

www.learnit-doit.com/cstemp10.html

www.ingramcontent.com/pod-product-compliance
Lightning Source LLC
LaVergne TN
LVHW051601070426
835507LV00021B/2697